GLADSTONE, DISRAELI
AND LATER
VICTORIAN POLITICS

Gladstone, Disraeli and Later Victorian Politics

THIRD EDITION

PAUL ADELMAN

LONGMAN
LONDON AND NEW YORK

Addison Wesley Longman Limited
Edinburgh Gate,
Harlow, Essex CM20 2JE,
United Kingdom
and Associated Companies throughout the world.

Published in the United States of America
by Addison Wesley Longman Inc., New York

First published 1970
Second Edition 1983
Twelfth impression 1995
Third Edition 1997

ISBN 0 582 293227

British Library Cataloguing in Publication Data

A catalogue record for this book is
available from the British Library

Library of Congress Cataloging-in-Publication Data
Adelman, Paul.
    Gladstone, Disraeli, and later Victorian politics / Paul Adelman.
-- 3rd ed.
    p. cm. -- (Seminar studies in history)
Includes bibliographical references and index.
ISBN 0-582-29322-7 (pbk. : alk. paper)
1. Great Britain -- Politics and government -- 1837–1901. 2. Gladstone, W. E.
(William Ewart), 1809–1898. 3. Disraeli, Benjamin, Earl of Beaconsfield,
1804–1881. 4. Political parties-Great Britain--History. 5. Conservative Party (Great
Britain) 6. Liberal Party (Great Britain) I. Title. II. Series.
DA560.A66 1996
320.941'09'034--dc20   96-29168
                                                                  CIP

Set by 7 in Sabon
Produced through Longman Malaysia, LSP

CONTENTS

For David and Juliet

EDITORIAL FOREWORD

Such is the pace of historical enquiry in the modern world that there is an ever-widening gap between the specialist article or monograph, incorporating the results of current research, and general surveys, which inevitably become out of date. *Seminar Studies in History* are designed to bridge this gap. The books are written by experts in their field who are not only familiar with the latest research but have often contributed to it. They are frequently revised, in order to take account of new information and interpretations. They provide a selection of documents to illustrate major themes and provoke discussion, and also a guide to further reading. Their aim is to clarify complex issues without over-simplifying them, and to stimulate readers into deepening their knowledge and understanding of major themes and topics.

NOTE ON REFERENCING SYSTEM

Readers should note that numbers in square brackets [5] refer them to the corresponding entry in the Bibliography at the end of the book (specific page numbers are given in italics). A number in square brackets preceded by *Doc.* [*Doc.* 5] refers readers to the corresponding item in the Documents section which follows the main text.

FOREWORD

The period between 1867 and the death of Queen Victoria in 1901 saw the development of the major features of the modern British political system, features which, in their essentials, still govern our political life today. It was during this period that the Second and Third Reform Acts of 1867 and 1884 established the principle of 'one man, one vote' and thus inaugurated the era of democratic politics; while the Redistribution Act of 1885, by dividing up the country into mainly one-member constituencies roughly equal in population, destroyed the old parliamentary map of Britain, and laid down the main outlines of the present constituency system. These changes in the electoral system at the centre were underpinned by the 'democratisation' of local government by the great acts of 1888 and 1894. Nor was electoral procedure left untouched. Corruption, bribery and influence had long disgraced the electoral scene even after the passing of the Second Reform Act, and despite the introduction of the secret ballot in 1872. But the passing of a rigorous Corrupt Practices Act in 1883 did much to destroy the evils of the old order, and helped to produce an electoral system that, within a generation, was reasonably fair and honest.

Above all, however, the period between 1867 and 1901 saw the development of the two-party system, associated with the 'swing of the pendulum' between the Liberal and Conservative (and later the Labour and Conservative) parties, that many people came to see as the essential and characteristic feature of modern British politics. It was this system too that produced and nourished the political giants of the age – Gladstone, Disraeli, Chamberlain, Salisbury – and helped to establish their hold over the political imagination of the British people, both then and since. But the Liberal and Conservative Parties in the later Victorian period were not just parliamentary organisations. Faced, after 1867, with the problem of winning working-class votes, both parties developed central organisations whose tasks – raising money, encouraging voluntary workers, finding suitable parliamentary candidates – were basically what they are today; while at the same time local constituency associations were developed which still remain important centres of local political life. Moreover, the federation of these local associations into great national organisations – the Conservative National Union of 1867, and the National Liberal Federation of 1877 – raised in an acute form the problem of the relationship between the parliamentary parties and extra-parliamentary opinion; a problem which, though scotched by the party leaders in the later nineteenth century, later emerged in a more virulent form to tax their successors.

This book is an attempt to describe the development of that later Victorian political system. It is concerned primarily with the two great parties, Liberal and Conservative, considered mainly as political organisations – vote-winning agencies – rather than as repositories of political ideas or vehicles of legislative change. It discusses, therefore, such problems as: how were the parties organised, who supported them and why, what factors divided and united them, what was the influence of leadership and policy upon their development, how successful or unsuccessful were they at general elections and why? This is not to deny the role of ideas in history or to insist that politics is just organisation; but it is an attempt to provide a guiding thread through a mass of historical detail, and to draw attention to aspects of nineteenth-century history which have received scant attention in the textbooks. For indeed it is in the field of party history in the later nineteenth century that some of the most interesting and fruitful work has been done by British and American historians in the last twenty years. Unfortunately, though, no general survey of the years 1867 to 1901 has been produced by a professional historian since R. C. K. Ensor published his *England 1870–1914* in 1936. This makes the study of the period challenging, but also, I believe, particularly rewarding for students, and especially well adapted to the seminar method of study. Many of the topics dealt with in this book are the concern of social scientists as well as historians. But this is intended to be an historical study. Though I have not, I hope, neglected the work of sociologists and political scientists, I have made no attempt to apply sociological 'theories' to the political world of the late Victorians. I have allowed the Victorians – the great and the insignificant – to speak for themselves; the student must draw his or her own conclusions.

Paul Adelman, 1970

Note on the Second Edition

I have taken the opportunity of a second edition to correct misprints and inaccuracies in the original text, and to expand on some points where brevity displaced understanding. My main purpose, however, has been to update the book in terms of the scholarship of the past decade, years which have seen the continuing publication of important works on later Victorian politics. The decade has on the whole been one of consolidation rather than of pioneering in historical writing. This is recognised by the recent publication of two new general surveys of the period by Professors Shannon and Read to compliment Ensor's classic textbook which (as my original Foreword records) for so long held the field.

Paul Adelman, 1982

Note on the Third Edition

The main purpose of this new edition is to take account of the more important books and articles published on later Victorian politics since the second edition of 1982. The last twelve years or so have in fact been outstanding for scholarly work in this field. In particular, they have seen the publication of original and stimulating studies of Gladstone and the development of the Liberal Party, by historians such as H. C. G. Matthew, Jonathan Parry, T. A. Jenkins and Eugenio Biagini. In addition, Richard Shannon has covered the history of the late Victorian Conservative Party in two volumes: *The Age of Disraeli, 1868–1881* (Longman, 1992), and *The Age of Salisbury, 1881–1902* (Longman, 1996). Some sections of the original work have therefore been largely rewritten.

Paul Adelman, 1996

PART ONE: THE SETTING

1 GLADSTONE'S LIBERAL PARTY

EARLY DEVELOPMENT

The origin of the Liberal Party is usually found in the famous meeting held in Willis's rooms on 6 June 1859, when the Whig, Peelite and Radical leaders in Parliament, drawn together by a common sympathy with Italy, agreed to combine together to expel the minority Conservative government of Derby and Disraeli. As a result, a new Liberal ministry was formed under Lord Palmerston, which contained for the first time both Gladstone and Lord John Russell. But the government of Lord Palmerston, which lasted for the next six years until his death in October 1865, was still basically only a reconstituted Whig ministry (it contained only one Radical) and indeed received the tacit support of the Conservative Party. Palmerston's death, however, marked something of a turning point in British political history. A Parliamentary Reform Bill, which the old statesman had long opposed, now became inevitable as Pam's successor, Lord John Russell, had long been an advocate of parliamentary reform and he was now supported over this by his outstanding, younger colleague, W. E. Gladstone.

The Reform Bill which the two Liberal leaders proposed in the spring of 1866 was a very moderate measure, which aimed to enfranchise only a small section of the better-off members of the urban working classes by lowering the borough franchise from ten-pound to seven-pound householders. But even this limited proposal was too much for some Liberal backbenchers; and a group of them, led by Robert Lowe, dubbed the Adullamites, combined with the Tory opposition in June 1866 to defeat the Bill. This was followed by the resignation of Russell and the coming into power of another minority Conservative government headed by Lord Derby and Disraeli. As a result of the brilliant tactics of Disraeli, it was the Conservatives who eventually pushed through the Reform Bill in the summer of 1867, a Bill which was a much more democratic measure than the original Liberal proposal since it was based on the principle of 'household suffrage'. This was (in Derby's phrase) the famous 'leap in the dark'. The Reform Act of 1867 added about a million new voters to the electorate, most of them workingmen who now became a majority of the voters in urban constituencies.

The passage of the Second Reform Act was soon followed by the retirement of Lord John Russell and the succession of Gladstone to the Liberal leadership. Early in 1868 Lord Derby also retired and Disraeli became Conservative Prime Minister. But his period of power was short-lived. In the spring of that year Gladstone introduced a series of resolutions into the House of Commons in favour of the disestablishment of the Church of Ireland, one of the pillars of the Protestant Ascendancy in that country, which were passed by comfortable majorities against the opposition of the government. The inevitable result was the dissolution of Parliament followed later that year by a general election.

Gladstone's motives in introducing his original resolutions were, as often, a mixture of idealism and political shrewdness. Though he was moved by a sense of 'justice for Ireland', he also hoped that his action would serve to re-unite the Liberal Party after the divisions over parliamentary reform in 1866–67, and help him to regain the political initiative from Disraeli. Opposition to religious privilege was a subject on which all Liberals could unite. Moreover, he believed that with the enlarged electorate created by the Second Reform Act, Irish Church reform would appeal not only to Roman Catholics but also to nonconformists and workingmen throughout Great Britain, many of whom were opposed to the privileges of the Church of England. Gladstone's expectations were largely fulfilled. Though religion was not the only factor at work, in the general election of November 1868 the Liberals, united and confident, were swept into power with a majority of more than a hundred and Gladstone formed his first Ministry. The Liberal Party had come of age.

The Parliamentary Liberal Party which thus came into existence in the 1860s bore all the marks of its origins. It was less a party in the modern sense – organised, disciplined, united around a programme – than a loose alliance of groups of many shades of opinion, reminiscent rather of the parliamentary 'connections' of the age of George III, than of the marshalled party battalions of today. The most famous of these groups, usually regarded as forming the extreme right wing of the party, was the Whigs [76]. A clique of wealthy aristocratic landowners, easygoing, affable and frank, but suspicious of what they did not understand, the Liberalism of the Whig grandees of the period was the product rather of tradition, habit and loyalty than of deeply felt ideas or principles. Indeed, they prided themselves on their commonsense and freedom from dogma. 'A Whig', said one of their number, 'has no fear of the people or of party cries. He merely says of all reforms "Prove your case and I will go with you..." '[53 p. 8]. The Whigs then were not as reactionary as has often been made out; and they saw themselves as an important and necessary element within the Liberal Party, a view which has been commended by a number of recent historians [53; 69]. In the classic description of Lord Hartington, their outstanding leader during the Gladstonian period, given in a public speech in 1883: the Whigs 'have formed a connecting link between the advanced party [the Radicals] and those classes which, possessing property, power and influence, are naturally averse to change'. They had ensured, he added, that necessary reforms came about 'by the calm and peaceful process of constitutional acts'[47, i pp. 405–6].

The importance of the Whigs lay not in their numbers, for though they were a large and important corps in the House of Lords, they formed only a small section of the Parliamentary Liberal Party in the Lower House in the 1860s; nor in their wealth – which though enormous was hardly tapped at all in the service of the Liberal Party. The Whigs embodied, it has been said, 'a tradition of aristocratic leadership' [53 p. 3]. Their real importance lay, therefore, in their domination of government – their virtual monopoly of many of the key posts in any Liberal ministry – and the extraordinary esteem of their colleagues and the Parliamentary Party.

At the opposite end of the party's spectrum were the Radicals, that is, those MPs who were committed to fundamental reform, political, religious and social [1]. They too, like the genuine Whigs in the Commons, were a small group – only about fifty members – though on specific reform proposals, particularly in relation to religion, they could generally count on considerably more support. The Radicals contained intellectuals like Henry Fawcett and John Stuart Mill, who sat briefly for Westminster from 1865 to 1868; but their most important constituent was the great nonconformist manufacturing interest, containing men like Samuel Morley, Titus Salt, William Rathbone and – greatest of all – John Bright, who represented mainly the new industrial constituencies in the North and Midlands. The radical group was the one section of the Liberal Party which was genuinely and passionately committed to challenging the established order in both church and state; and, in this respect, their greatest obstacle was not so much the glittering but tiny array of Whigs, but the pedestrian mass of moderate Liberals who, neither Whig nor Radical, formed the bulk of the membership of the Parliamentary Liberal Party. The moderate Liberals were the ballast which every great parliamentary party must contain. Landowners, lawyers, gentlemen of leisure, army and naval officers, their background and attitudes made them distrustful of 'enthusiasm' in either religion or politics, and inclined them therefore to be a cautious, but a reasonably openminded, force within the party. In these ways they had much in common with the Whigs. Nor is this surprising, since most of the moderate MPs were associated with landed society in one way or another and a number of them were directly related to the Whig aristocracy. It has been estimated that about 60 per cent of members of the Parliamentary Liberal Party in the 1860s belonged to the landed classes, while only about 16 per cent were members of the commercial and industrial classes [54 *pp. 126–7*]. On the whole, the moderates were content to accept the platitudes of contemporary Liberalism and follow the lead of the more distinguished men on the Liberal Front Bench. And indeed this was the major purpose of the Parliamentary Liberal Party as a whole: to sustain the power of a leadership which, in a rough and ready way, skimmed the cream of the administrative talent available in the Liberal ranks in both Houses of Parliament. It was this belief that Administration is the highest form of politics – the greatest legacy of the Peelites to the Liberals – that helped to make the governing hierarchy of the Liberal Party in the age of Gladstone something of a distinct group within, but also apart from, the Parliamentary Party; a group with its own traditions, its own loyalties, and its own code of disinterested, efficient and highminded service.

The meeting at Willis's rooms, however, and the development of the Parliamentary Liberal Party, is only one side of the story of Liberalism in the 1860s. What is much more important, John Vincent has argued in an important book, is the growth of change – not at the centre – but at the grass roots; the development of new social forces in the country at large which looked to the Parliamentary Liberal Party for leadership and expression. What were these new social forces? There were, Vincent suggests, three: the creation of a cheap daily provincial Press, the growth of militant nonconformity, and the rise of organised labour [80].

The rise of a popular Press in the mid–Victorian years was one of the great silent social revolutions of the age. The repeal of the stamp and paper duties between 1855 and 1861 – together with the railway, the telegraph and the steam press – enabled the cheap provincial Press to make a great leap forward in both number of newspapers and circulation, and thus destroy the exclusive metropolitan domination of the 'respectable' newspapers like *The Times* [10]. Moreover, this new provincial Press was dominated mainly by local Liberal politicians, such as the Baines family with the *Leeds Mercury*, the Cowens' *Newcastle Chronicle*, and the Leader family's *Sheffield Independent*. These men used their papers for Liberal – often radical – proselytisation, and helped to build up, therefore, an articulate, self–conscious, provincial Liberalism which became one of the pillars of the new Liberal Party.

Another pillar was militant nonconformity [*Doc. 1*]. The nonconformist community as a whole, with the notable exception of the Wesleyans, had always of course traditionally looked towards the old Whig party as the opponents of that exclusive Anglicanism that marked their Tory rivals. That allegiance was now potentially available to the Liberal Party also, as the best instrument through which the nonconformists could realise those special religious, social and educational reforms, which could transform the purely legal equality granted to them in 1828 into practical reality. They had obtained some minor concessions from the Whig governments in the 1830s. But what they now wanted was the abolition of compulsory church rate paid to the Church of England, and the end of the Anglican monopoly at the universities of Oxford and Cambridge, as well as a dimunition of Anglican influence within the school system. Some militant nonconformist leaders went further. For men such as Edward Miall – editor of the *Nonconformist* and Liberal MP – no real advance towards religious equality could be expected while the Church of England remained as the Established Church of the land. Only the disestablishment and disendowment of the Church of England could really destroy the nonconformists' status as second-class citizens. This was the major aim of the 'Liberation Society' which was organised by Miall and other militant colleagues in 1853. By the 1860s it had become the most famous and the most powerful of the great nonconformist pressure groups which aimed at influencing national and parliamentary opinion in their favour [1; 3].

The nonconformists believed they were in a position to make their weight felt. For they were now a dynamic, militant, wealthy and expanding community – the great Religious Census of 1851 had shown that about half the churchgoing population of the kingdom belonged to the nonconformist communities. Their strength was concentrated mainly in the great industrial cities of the North of England, scattered communities in the West and East Anglia, and in Wales where nonconformity eventually came to dominate the religious life of the people [18]. Socially, support came mainly from the middle classes and the artisans. The nonconformists were prepared to place their wealth, their votes – a bloc of 87 nonconformist MPs was returned at the general election of 1865 – together with their influence, their zeal and their organising ability at the disposal of the Liberal Party in return for the fond – but as it turned out largely delusive – expectation that the Parliamentary Party would foster their special interests. Thus began that peculiar love–hate relationship between the Liberal Establishment and the nonconformist world which lasted until, in the early twentieth century, the power of organised nonconformity declined, and with it, eventually, the Liberal Party itself [42; 3].

As with the nonconformists, so with the new working–class elite of trade union leaders and skilled artisans who were prospering with the mid–Victorian boom. Emancipation for them too could be expressed by supporting and voting for the Liberal Party: not only in the sense that, like the nonconformists, they had special interests to achieve – over trade union rights, taxes, hours of work – but in a more profound political and psychological way. 'To vote Liberal', as Vincent suggests, 'was closely tied to the growing ability of whole new classes to stand on their own feet' [80 p. xiv]. Working–class Liberalism was thus not entirely, or even mainly, based on simple economic motivation, and the provincial industrial workers were often at one with their masters in their support for the Liberal cause against the forces represented locally by Squire and Parson. Indeed, questions of personal status and subtle pressures *within* a local urban community were as much the determinants of Liberal allegiance generally, as the more overt economic and religious grievances [134; 154].

In the 1860s, therefore, the Parliamentary Liberal Party became of major importance in the political life of the country because it established links with these new dynamic forces in the nation at large. The man who saw their importance and carried through this liaison, who used these great religious and social movements to breathe life into the dry bones of the Parliamentary Liberal Party, was W. E. Gladstone. By doing so he was able to assert an almost unquestioned personal ascendancy over them all for the next twenty years, and his inspiration continued long after his death.

Yet Gladstone had begun his political life at the time of the Great Reform Bill of 1832 as a vigorous High Churchman and Tory, and it was not until the later 1840s and the 1850s, by which time he was the outstanding leader of the Peelites in the House of Commons, that he started seriously to reconsider his early opinions. Even so, as Shannon and other historians have stressed, he was never able to shake off completely the influence of his early Tory beliefs [49; 68; 74]. What pushed Gladstone towards Liberalism during this period was the collapse of his belief in the union of church and state and the acceptance of the notion of religious freedom and civil equality for all groups and sects. Under the influence of Sir Robert Peel – in whose great Ministry of 1841–46 he had served as President of the Board of Trade – he also came to believe that the free enterprise system, based on *laissez-faire* and free trade, would best lead to economic growth and prosperity for all sections of the community. Finally, Gladstone was now strongly influenced by the principle of nationality, particularly in relation to Italy, and in the 1850s he became more and more sympathetic to the cause of Italian unity and freedom. It was in fact the Italian question, on which the two statesmen more or less saw eye to eye, that helped Gladstone to overcome his suspicions of Lord Palmerston – whose bellicose foreign policy he had bitterly denounced a generation earlier – and join his new Liberal government in 1859. He was also tired of being out of office and profoundly concious of his own abilities and ambitions. 'I saw great things to do', he noted in his Diary, 'particularly in the field of finance and trade' [63, i *p. 106].* He therefore accepted with alacrity the post of Chancellor of the Exchequer in 1859, a position he held until the summer of 1866.

Gladstone's great free trade budgets of the early 1860s were decisive in his career. They not only won him the support of the commercial and manufacturing interests and the working classes in the country, but also established his authority in Parliament and his indispensability to the government [63, i]. They also led though, owing to the way in which he stood up to both the Prime Minister and the House of Lords over his Paper Bill, to murmurings on the right wing of the Liberal bloc: 'The Whigs hate Gladstone', wrote Sir Robert Phillimore in 1860; and one of the greatest of that clan, Lord Clarendon, described the Chancellor as 'an audacious innovator with an insatiable desire of popularity . . . his ungratified personal vanity makes him wish to subvert the institutions and classes that .stand in the way of his ambition' [76 *p. 299].* Indeed,

Gladstone's independent stance in the government made him no more popular in the House than he had been in his Peelite days. Now, however, it mattered less, since, as Gladstone began to observe with increasing satisfaction, a mass opinion was being built up outside the House of Commons which moved gradually but inexorably towards him as its parliamentary spokesman. For the repeal of the paper duties – the 'taxes on knowledge' – not only helped to reinforce a middle–class provincial Liberalism based on a cheap Press, it helped also to sponsor a working–class Liberalism – to educate the country's future masters.

Indeed, the main theme of Gladstone's political life in the early 1860s is his fairly steady move to the left, much to the dismay of the Prime Minister [39]. What this now meant in practical terms was an increasing respect for and sympathy with the aspirations of the skilled workingmen and, to some extent, the nonconformists. And both cause and effect of this was Gladstone's growing awareness of his superb power as a mass orator to move men, as seen in his great tours of the North of England. To win over these new national forces Gladstone quite deliberately, and successfully, used the publicity resources of the time: the great mass meeting, which he made peculiarly his own, especially in the industrial areas, and the Press, where he made sure that his speeches were reported in detail. Here he relied particularly on the new, cheap newspaper – price, one penny – *The Daily Telegraph*, which had a large circulation, rather than the quality newspapers such as *The Times* [10]. Gladstone wrote in his Diary after one such tour in the North in October 1864: 'So ended in peace an exhausting, flattering . . . circuit. God knows I have not courted them. . . . It is, however, impossible not to love the people from whom such manifestations come as meet me at every quarter . . . ' [66, i *p. 76*]. It was not that Gladstone had any real understanding of the life of the ·working–class audiences he addressed, nor, as he insisted, much to offer them directly that would mitigate the harshness of their lives. But what he could do with his inspiring oratory (which reads so tortuously today) was to raise their status as human beings, to bring them into touch, albeit vicariously, with the wider, dramatic political conflicts of the age at home and abroad.

By the mid–1860s Gladstone was convinced that the British workers' attitude, as shown by their fortitude in Lancashire during the cotton famine, produced by the American Civil War, their build–up of the great craft unions and friendly societies, and their support for his new savings banks and other financial reforms, was, as he said, 'one of confidence in the law, in parliament, even in the executive government' [82 *p. 57*]. The outcome of this new conviction was his famous declaration in May 1864: 'I venture to say that every man who is not presumably incapacitated by some consideration of personal unfitness or of political danger, is morally entitled to come within the pale of the constitution' [66, i *p. 760*]. It is true that under the prompting of Palmerston, Gladstone did put a more conservative gloss on the words. But the democratic implications were unmistakable, and were drawn increasingly by the working people who saw him more and more as 'the People's William'. A group of Yorkshire textile workers spoke for many members of their class when, in an address to Gladstone at this time, they wrote:

We have marked your manifestations of sympathy with the down-trodden and oppressed of every clime. . . . To the provident operative you have by your Post Office Savings Bank bill given security for his small savings. . . . These acts, together with your speeches on the Borough Franchise bill, make up a life that commands our lasting gratitude. [66, i *pp. 764–5*]

For workingmen, the cult of Gladstone as 'the Charismatic Leader' developed apace during this period. It has been argued by E. Biagini that this adulation was based primarily on hard, material facts [27]. Popular radicals – the heirs of a long tradition going back to the early nineteenth century and beyond – strongly approved of lower government expenditure and lower taxation. They admired what Gladstone had done so far for the members of their class by introducing free trade and financial reform, and they looked forward expectantly to the 'free breakfast table' – the ending of the remaining taxes on working-class foodstuffs. They also hoped for an improved system of income tax. Nevertheless, Gladstone's appeal to the masses was based as much, if not more, on moral and emotional factors; and Biagini himself, in his recent study of popular radicalism during the Gladstonian period, provides much evidence for this [28]. Typical was one workingman's description of Gladstone speaking at a public meeting in the 1860s:

Without an effort – so it seemed to me – the great orator held his audience for nearly 2 hours. I stood so far off that the features were indistinct but was spellbound by the music and magnetism of the wonderful voice. . . . I was only conscious of the presence of a great human personality under whose spell I was, and from whom I could in no way escape. . . . I felt lifted into a holy region of politics. . . . [28 *pp. 390–1*]

We can see a similar rapport developing between Gladstone and the nonconformists. 'A liberal and kindly treatment of the Church of England by the State and of dissenters by the Church is what I desire', he said [20 *p. 325*]. The nonconformists in turn came to see Gladstone as the great Liberal statesman who accepted their fundamental desire for civil equality and supported their specific demands to achieve this. They were impressed by his support for 'democracy' during the last years of Palmerston's government, and by his condemnation of the Anglican Establishment in Ireland. Above all, they came to see Gladstone as a man who had the same powerful belief as themselves in the moral basis of politics. As one nonconformist editor wrote of him: 'Dissenters have confidence in the deep feeling of religiousness which appears to imbue your public life and to make it a great and sacred responsibility' [58 *p. 358*].

In the general election of 1865 Gladstone's fellow-travelling with democracy and dissent lost him his seat at Oxford University; but he stood for South Lancashire. 'At last my friends', he said in a speech at Manchester, 'I am come among you, and I am come among you "unmuzzled" ' [66, i *p. 358*], the famous remark which seems to sum up, politically and psychologically, Gladstone's development in the 1860s. In the course of the next two years he was able to establish even more closely that favour with the masses which enabled him to emerge, despite Disraeli's tactical victory, as the real hero of 1867, and, in the following year, Prime Minister.

The importance of all this is enormous. What Gladstone helped to achieve in the 1860s and early 1870s was to win over to the Liberal Party the vast majority of the working-class electors, and the nonconformists. In this way he helped to make the Liberal Party a national party, and indeed a classless party, which aimed to appeal to all classes and thus help to reduce the barriers between them. This point serves to underline the way in which Gladstone led the Liberal Party. For one of the main problems that faced the Liberals during this, and indeed later periods, was how to maintain unity within a Parliamentary Party which was more or less a coalition of different groups and interests: workers and employers, Whigs and Radicals, Anglicans and nonconformists. Unity was maintained not primarily through political organisation, not even through political programmes, but mainly through Gladstone's claim to be 'above' the Liberal groups by virtue of his links with the masses. As Vincent says: 'Gladstone ruled Parliament through the electorate. He was a Minister given by the people to the Party' [80 *p. 227*].

What then did Liberalism come to mean for Gladstone during his years of political ascendancy? At the centre of Gladstone's Liberalism was his religion [46; 49]. It was a sense of religious mission that had first impelled him towards the House of Commons in the early 1830s. He believed profoundly that politics was or should be a field of Christian action. This comes out even in his views on the free enterprise system, which he said rested upon 'religion and Christian virtue . . . as the means of creating and preserving wealth' [74 *p. 124*] It meant too that his foreign policy was governed by his notion of 'the law of nations': a public law overriding selfish national interests and committing the civilised nations of the world to work together for peace and mutual understanding [116]. It was this ideal that led him during his First Ministry to support the 'Alabama' award to the United States, and condemn the claim of Prussia to Alsace–Lorraine after the defeat of France in 1870–71. Even more important was Gladstone's conception of 'freedom', which for him was a positive ideal of self–fulfilment and moral development, for nations as well as individuals. How then could a Christian and a Liberal ignore the demand for freedom of a people 'rightly struggling to be free'? In such a situation – whether over Bulgaria in 1876, or Ireland in the 1880s – driven by the creation of what he called a 'virtuous passion', Gladstone threw caution to the winds and was prepared to abandon everything else for the successful pursuance of this great Christian ideal. On such occasions he became incapable of moderation and almost believed – like Cromwell – that God was working through him, and the multitudes who followed where he led. The second source of Gladstone's Liberalism is virtually the corollary of the first. Gladstone was a great 'popular' statesman because he became more and more convinced in the 1870s and 1880s of the 'selfishness' of the upper classes and the 'goodness' of the masses. Who, after all, consistently opposed him over Bulgaria and Ireland – and why? 'The burden of his song', wrote a fellow Liberal in 1871, 'is always the deterioration of the Governing Classes in comparison with the poor. He said very solemnly that our Lord's teaching goes very deep in this direction as to the poor being better and wiser than the rich' [80 *p. 216*]. By 1880 this had become the semi–mystical belief that a special *rapport* existed between himself and the people, united together against the unwavering hostility of the Victorian Establishment. Nowhere is this feeling expressed more vividly than in his great speech at West Calder during the Midlothian Campaign [*Doc. 2*]. It was this extraordinary juxtaposition of alien elements, and especially his passionate moralism, that gave Gladstone his strength and weakness in politics. Everyone admits his dominating personality, his remarkable powers of work, his administrative gifts, his supreme oratorical powers both in the Commons and outside, and his command of popular aspirations. But he was also – perhaps because of these gifts, as A. F. Thompson suggests – a bad party leader and party manager, tactless and awkward with many of his colleagues, and neglecting vital issues both of policy and organisation in order to pursue, ruthlessly and relentlessly, his personal crusades [79]. Another historian has recently wondered whether Gladstone can really be considered a Liberal at all. Jonathan Parry has suggested that Gladstone's temperament and his moralistic, emotional, populist style of politics set him apart from the rational, consensual, parliamentary tradition of politics which marked the evolution of the Whig–Liberal party from the 1830s onwards [69]. Certainly, some of Gladstone's colleagues would have sympathised with this point of view. The former Lord Chancellor, Lord Selbourne, writing after the fall of Gladstone's First Ministry in 1874, considered that 'his mind seems to me to be too one-sided and vehement, and to want accuracy, equability and a sense of proportion ... he does not sympathise, or take counsel with, those whose point of view is at all different from his own' [*54 p. 141*].

Much of this, however, lay in the future. After the great electoral victory of 1868, the Liberal Party was more popular and more united than it was ever to be again in the nineteenth century, and Gladstone's personal position was assured. His first government has been called by Ensor 'the greatest ministry of Victoria's reign' [*5 p. 26*]; but its successes were due more to the *élan* that affected the whole party in those early hopeful years, and the topics tackled, than to the outstanding abilities of the ministers as a whole. The government was very much a 'mixed ministry', containing Whigs, Peelites and Radicals, but with the Whigs predominating. On the other hand, the new 'middle–class' ministers (not all of whom were Radicals) controlled internal departments with important legislative responsibilities: Bright at the Board of Trade, Lowe at the Treasury, H. A. Bruce at the Home Office, W. E. Forster in charge of Education, and Cardwell at the War Office. Together they formed, for Gladstone, 'one of the best instruments for government that ever was constructed' [*52 p. 293*].

It was the last three who were mainly responsible for the important, though long overdue, domestic reforms that were now passed: the changes in the civil service, the judiciary and the army; the great Education Act of 1870; the abolition of religious tests at Oxford and Cambridge (compulsory church rate had already been abolished by the Conservatives in 1868, mainly due to pressure from Gladstone); the Local Government and Trade Union Acts in 1871; and the introduction of the secret ballot in 1872, as well as Bruce's clumsy and unpopular Licensing Act, which attempted to regulate the opening hours of public houses.

Gladstone, though in general he approved of what was done, left the details of the Bills to his ministers. He himself was engrossed in the 'pacification' of Ireland, which he believed would be achieved through the passage of three great reforms – in religion, land and education. The passing of the Irish Church Act in 1869, which disestablished and disendowed the Church of Ireland, was a great personal triumph for the Prime Minister, and showed his qualities at their best. But the Irish Land Act of 1870, which aimed to improve the rights of the tenants, was largely a failure. The Irish Universities Bill, too, which Gladstone hoped would provide greater opportunities in higher education for the Catholics, was defeated in the House of Commons in 1873 and led, though only temporarily, to the Prime Minister's retirement. The fate of the Universities Bill, which was lost owing to the abstentions or negative votes of the Irish Liberal MPs, was symptomatic of the state of the Liberal Party at this time. By 1873, in fact, the uneasy coalition of forces that had won for the Liberals their remarkable victory in 1868 was split wide apart, and the seeds of disunity and disillusionment were already at work [Doc. 3]. How had this come about?

DECLINE

One of the major causes of Liberal disunity was the opposition of the nonconformists to Forster's 1870 Education Act [Doc. 4]. This Act not only failed to provide that system of free, national and secular education to which the nonconformists were now committed, but seemed to favour the Anglican religious schools by increasing their state grants and allowing them, through the notorious Clause 25, to obtain some measure of rate aid as well. The nonconformists had their own educational 'pressure group' in the form of the National Education League, founded at Birmingham in 1869 by Joseph Chamberlain and a group of local Radicals; and as a result of their detestation of the government's educational policy the activities of the League became more political and more extreme. 'With this knowledge of our opinions', wrote Chamberlain, 'the Government has chosen deliberately to defy us. ... This conduct leaves us no alternative. ... The great principle of religious equality must be accepted as part of the Programme of any Party which in future seeks our support and alliance. The "Nonconformist Revolt" long threatened has at last begun ' [41, i *p. 137*].

Underlying and reflecting these disputes over education were the profound differences that existed within the Liberal Party over religious matters. Parry has therefore argued that it was really religion that was the major cause of Liberal disunity during the early 1870s, and it was the religious tensions created by and within the Liberal Party that contributed to its dramatic defeat in the general election of 1874 [67]. For the rift between the nonconformists and the government over education was worsened as a result of the national campaign in favour of the disestablishment of the Church of England launched by the Liberation Society early in 1871, a direct response to the great Act of 1869 which had successfully disestablished the Anglican Church of Ireland. In May 1871 a 'grand inquest' on the subject was held in the House of Commons as a result of Edward Miall's motion in favour of the disestablishment of the Church of England. There was no chance of the motion succeeding, and both Gladstone and Disraeli strongly defended the religious *status quo*. The motion was lost by 374 votes to 89. Nevertheless, the fact that a large minority of nonconformists and Radicals voted in favour, exposed once again the growing disunity within the Liberal Party. There was also an undercurrent of anti-Roman Catholic feeling in the country which exacerbated the situation. This was due to the work of the Vatican Council of 1870, and particularly the promulgation of the decree on Papal Infallibility; the growth of ritualism within the Church of England; and (as we saw earlier) the introduction of Gladstone's Irish Universities Bill early in 1873, though that was in fact defeated mainly as a result of the opposition of the Irish Liberal MPs. That defeat symbolically marked the beginning of the end for the Liberal Party in Ireland, since that very year the Irish Home Rule Party was formed as a rival to the main English parties.

By 1873, a second great stream of discontent with the Liberal government had come to a head: the Trade Union Revolt had also begun. For in 1871 the government, following the Report of the

Royal Commission on Trade Unions set up in 1867, passed a new Trade Union Act. This gave the unions full legal recognition, but took away from them the right of 'peaceful picketing' by passing a separate Criminal Law Amendment Act which not only made unionists still liable to prosecution under the 1825 Act but, owing to an amendment added by the Lords, made the requirements of that Act even stricter. This attitude of the Liberal government was greeted with bitter resentment by the trade unions – especially after the infamous way in which the law was actually applied in various *causes célèbres* – and prompted great agitation for the repeal of the Amendment Act, led by the recently formed Trades Union Congress [172]. It was this agitation which, in the words of the Webbs, 'became during the next four years the most significant feature of the Trade Union World' [174 *p. 283*]; and, as a result, the labour movement became not only increasingly antipathetic to official Liberalism, but more politically minded and more independent.

The year 1873 was in fact a turning point in the history of the first Liberal administration. The great burst of reforms that marked its early years had now petered out. The government was rapidly losing the support of those vital forces – nonconformists, working men, Roman Catholics and Radicals – which had won it the notable victory of 1868, and becoming that 'range of exhausted volcanoes' of Disraeli's brilliant gibe. After his return as Prime Minister in the spring of 1873, Gladstone reflected sadly: 'There is now no great cause, no great public object on which the Liberal Party are agreed and combined' [63, i *p. 224*]. In the summer things got worse. Important by-elections were lost. Scandals were revealed in the administration of the Post Office and both the Postmaster-General and the Chancellor of the Exchequer were forced to resign. Gladstone, unwisely, then took over the Treasury himself in addition to his other burdens. On 22 October John Bright, in a speech to his constituents at Birmingham, denounced Clause 25 of the Education Act as 'an evil principle', and made a strong attack on those responsible for it; his fellow minister, W. E. Forster, replied a few days later at Liverpool and repudiated all that Bright had said [41, i *pp. 141–2*]. At the end of 1873, therefore, confusion, disunion and virtual despair reigned in the ranks of the Liberal government and Parliamentary Party.

By the new year, however, Gladstone had reached the decision to dissolve, and he believed that 'Repeal of the Income Tax' was an election cry which would win back public confidence and reunite the party. In addition, the refusal of the Service ministers, Cardwell and Goschen, to accept fully the proposed reduction in their estimates, provided the Prime Minister with 'that perfectly honourable difference of opinion' on the basis of which he could urge the Queen to dissolve. On 24 January 1874 the dissolution of Parliament was announced to a startled country. The National Education League was caught unprepared. The unexpected dissolution was described by the *Nonconformist* as 'a bolt from an unclouded sky which dished the Radicals' [144]. For the League had expected that the ministry would last another year, and the sudden dissolution shattered the morale of the nonconformist bloc. How were they to vote when faced with a Liberal candidate? The outcome of the general election of 1874 was an overall majority of fifty for Disraeli, and many League supporters went down to defeat, including Joseph Chamberlain at Sheffield. The trade union movement was better prepared, though in the end they were hardly more successful than the League – only two labour candidates were returned out of thirteen who stood.

Why then did the Liberal Party lose the election? Much has been made of the 'Nonconformist Revolt'. Francis Adams, the historian of the League, estimated that about twenty seats were lost to the Liberals through nonconformist abstentions at the polls [22], but it seems fairly certain that the importance of the League generally as an influence in the Liberal débâcle has been exaggerated. Nonconformist voters were, after all, as Professor Hanham has emphasised, concentrated in the under–represented cities of the North and Midlands [135]; and though there were a large number of seats – thirty-four – where unauthorised Liberals stood owing to party divisions, Arthur Peel, the Liberal Chief Whip, estimated that only thirteen were lost due to those divisions [144]. For the education issue was only one, and not perhaps the most important issue, in the election. 'We have been borne down in a torrent of gin and beer', said Gladstone in a phrase which has stuck [66, ii p. 103], and the 'brewers' revolt' – in opposition to the Licensing Act of 1872 – though its effects have been exaggerated, was an important factor. Even more important was working–class opposition to the Criminal Law Amendment Act. 'The law of conspiracy is their 25th clause', as Frederic Harrison, the Radical, shrewdly said; and some trade unionists probably abstained, following the advice given by their leaders, and some probably voted Conservative. Parry has stressed the importance of religious issues in the general election, and especially the fears in the country that the Liberal Party was now identified with disestablishment and opposition to religious education in schools, owing to pressure from the nonconformists and Radicals [67]. But these issues are best seen, perhaps, as evidence of a wider, middle-class disenchantment with Gladstonian Liberalism. For the most important reason of all for the Liberal defeat was, quite simply, the swing of the middle-class voter, alarmed by the rise of the working classes in strength and influence and increasingly conscious of his own status as 'a man of property', to the Conservative Party, particularly in suburbia, as all sections of political society recognised [*Doc. 6*]. And all these factors were worsened for the disunited Liberal Party by the raggedness of its party organisation compared with that of its opponents.

2 DISRAELI'S CONSERVATIVE PARTY

THE SECOND REFORM ACT

The policy of Sir Robert Peel in trying to provide a more progressive ethos for his party in the early nineteenth century ground to a halt in 1846. By 1865, after twenty years in the wilderness under the leadership of the Earl of Derby in the Lords and, more precariously, Disraeli in the Commons, little had been done to provide the Conservative Party with new supporters, new policies or new enthusiasm [115]. What changed the outlook for the party was the death of Palmerston. 'The truce of parties is over', proclaimed Disraeli, ' I foresee tempestuous times, and great vicissitudes in public life' [115 p. 352]. He was right. Pam's death produced a more 'fluid' situation after years of torpor, and the possibility therefore of a realignment of political forces from which the Conservatives could benefit. The events of 1866 – the introduction of the Liberal Reform Bill, the Adullamite revolt, the defeat of the Bill – produced just such a situation, and led in June to the establishment of a minority Conservative government under Derby and Disraeli. The motives that now governed the Conservative leaders, and the tactics that were pursued by Disraeli especially, in the course of the next twelve months down to the passing of the final Act, have been analysed in almost microscopic detail by a group of recent historians [17; 21; 166]. As a result, a whole political mythology has been virtually destroyed. It is now clear that Disraeli's attitude during the Reform Crisis was purely opportunist. He neither sought to 'educate his party', nor displayed either firmness or consistency of purpose in his support for 'democracy'. Indeed, during these months Disraeli had only one major aim: to destroy Gladstone's leadership over a united Liberal Party, and, by seizing the initiative in reform himself and promoting a Reform Bill, to raise the fortunes of the Conservative Party and consolidate his own position as a party leader. The latter point is particularly important in view of Disraeli's tenuous hold over the party in the Commons in the 1850s. For, as Maurice Cowling has argued, Disraeli's brilliant tactical success in 1867 was not just a victory over Gladstone and the Liberals; it was as much a personal victory within his own party. It meant 'that Derby and Disraeli were going to run the Conservative Party, not Cranborne and Peel, and that those elements in the party which wanted to get rid of Disraeli would have to destroy the party in the process' [17 *p. 164*]. Why did the party follow Disraeli? Not only, suggests Cowling, for party advantage, but because the final Act itself had 'conservative' as well as 'democratic' implications. It is the 'conservative' aspect of the Second Reform Act that is of fundamental importance in considering the position of the Conservative Party after 1867.

To many contemporaries, both of the Left and the Right, the Second Reform Act seemed to be an essentially democratic measure which gave effective political power to the working class. Superficially this appeared to be true. Nearly a million new voters were added to the electoral list, and the increase was widest in the great cities where working-class voters now became a majority. But the position in the counties was very different, and does much to justify Cowling's remark that Disraeli 'was prepared to let Radicals have their way in the boroughs, so long as he had his to some extent in the counties' [17 *p. 233*]. For in the counties the vote was given only to the twelve-pound householders, a deferential group, which meant that the number of voters rose only from 540,000 to 790,000 – an increase of only 40 per cent compared with a 134 per cent increase in the boroughs. In addition, since in county areas the rural districts were strongly reinforced by boundary changes, which deliberately lopped off suburban areas and added them to the boroughs, conditions there were not very much different after 1867. In the counties, therefore, the old order continued almost undisturbed, and they remained the chief stronghold of the Conservative Party which, in the later nineteenth century, regularly won in them twice as many seats as its opponents [135].

In any case the question of the franchise, from a long-term point of view, was not the most important aspect of the Reform Act. Much more significant was what Bright called 'the very soul of the question of reform' – the problem of redistribution. Here, the 'conservative' nature of the Bill was even more clearly evident. For in England and Wales only fifty-two seats were redistributed in 1867, and twenty-five of these went to the counties to enlarge an already conservative franchise; while the four greatest provincial cities – Manchester, Birmingham, Leeds and Liverpool – were fobbed off with an extra member, bringing their representation up to only three members each. This lack of a fundamental redistribution of seats meant that not only were Liberal votes piled up and wasted in the great centres of population, whereas Conservative votes were more evenly distributed throughout the country, but that many of the old anomalies remained. After 1867 there were still more than seventy boroughs with a population of less than 10,000 voters, and the boroughs as a whole were still considerably over-represented. Hence many of the corrupt electoral habits of a previous political era were carried over into the post-Reform period; and, despite the Ballot Act of 1872, corruption, bribery and deference remained important features of the new electoral system for at least another generation. 'Disraeli's Reform Bill left the spirit of the ancient constitution unbreached' [110 *p. 11*].

What all this meant was that the Second Reform Act did not mark that fundamental break in English political life which its supporters had expected and its enemies dreaded. This did not come about until the 1880s. The year 1867 did not inaugurate an age of democracy; did not, in fact, give the working classes direct political power; no workingman, for example, was to be returned at the general election of 1868 [*Doc. 7*]. What it did was not to revolutionise the direction of government, but to produce a major transformation in the relationship of the electorate and government. In the light of these considerations, the Act of 1867 offered to the Conservative Party positive advantages both of policy and electoral strategy. Whether these advantages would be seized, and how they would be used, depended very much on the relationship between Disraeli, the Parliamentary Party and the new electorate.

DISRAELIAN CONSERVATISM

Disraeli became Prime Minister early in 1868 after Lord Derby's retirement. But his journey to the top of the greasy pole (in his own famous phrase) was by no means pre-destined. Ever since he had first been elected a Conservative MP in 1837 he had been mistrusted by the party rank-and-file as an outsider – a man who was not identified with any of the groups and interests within the Conservative Party. He became Conservative leader in the House of Commons in 1849 only as a result of the split in the party over the repeal of the Corn Laws, which left him as the outstanding parliamentarian on the opposition benches. As the diehard Tory, the

Duke of Newcastle, insisted: 'We must of necessity choose the cleverest man we possess' [115 *p. 234*]. But during the long years of opposition after 1849 Disraeli's personal position was by no means secure. He held the leadership (in Vincent's phrase) 'only on sufferance' [118 *p. 56*].

It is true of course (as we saw earlier) that Disraeli's role in the passing of the Second Reform Act gave an enormous boost to his reputation and made him Lord Derby's obvious successor. But even after he became Prime Minister in 1868, Disraeli's position was by no means completely assured [120]. His support for 'democracy' in 1867 had incurred the bitter opposition and distrust of the right wing of the party, led by its intellectual mentor, Robert Cecil, now Marquis of Salisbury. And, as Salisbury argued with virulent conviction, the electoral rout that soon followed was not only a sufficient condemnation of Disraeli's leadership, but a direct consequence of his 'grave political insincerity' [89]. Nor was the opposition solely reactionary and aristocratic. Conservative reformers like Cross and Sandon were also sceptical about Disraeli's effectiveness as a leader, a mood which was enhanced in many sections of the party by his refusal to take office in 1873. Moreover, the very magnitude of the Liberals' victory, and the reasonableness of many of their reform proposals, was bound to make effective opposition difficult for any Conservative leader. But Disraeli suffered further from the fact that his leadership was purely personal: he was not associated with any of the sections of the Conservative Party nor, unlike the Liberal leader, was he able to draw upon any great reserves of influence in the nation at large. The Conservatives, as Feuchtwanger suggests, were never Disraeli's party as the Liberals were Gladstone's [133]. His policy up to 1874, there-fore, aimed at ensuring his own political survival by exercising his rightful authority without upsetting too many Tory susceptibilities – and looking towards the future. This meant temporising over Liberal reforms, and then cashing in on the growing Liberal disunity and unpopularity they helped to produce. At the same time Disraeli outlined a general Conservative programme in his public speeches in 1872 which could appeal to all sections of the community; and he also concentrated on building up a superior party organisation.

It was these tactics that seemed to pay off in the general election of 1874, when the Conservatives made important gains in the boroughs and won an overall majority of fifty. It was this electoral victory – the first Conservative one since 1841 – rather than the events of 1867–68, which really made Disraeli master of the

Conservative Party. 'After thirty years of scorn and sullenness', as he observed of the Tory aristocracy, 'they have melted before time and events' [84]. This new *rapprochement*, and indeed the new forces affecting Conservatism, were seen when Disraeli formed his government. Inevitably, given the Prime Minister's predilection for the aristocracy, the Cabinet contained six peers, including Salisbury who thus re-entered the fold. But of much greater significance was the group of commoners, mainly middle-class men, who then or soon afterwards entered the government: R. A. Cross, a pillar of Lancashire Conservatism, who had never before held office, as Home Secretary; Lord Sandon, a member for Liverpool, in charge of education; Sclater-Booth at the Local Government Board; and W. H. Smith, first at the Admiralty and then at the Treasury. Thus the government was not only a strong one in its own right, it also represented all the important sections of the party. It was this that helped to keep the Conservatives steadily together for the next six years.

The task that faced the Conservative Party in power, as it had faced it since 1867, was how to win and maintain support among the new voters created by the Second Reform Act without antagonising its traditional supporters, and this depended mainly on the party's programme. What in fact was to be the basis of Disraelian Conservatism? The fundamental task of the Conservative Party, Disraeli had written earlier, was 'to uphold the aristocratic settlement of the country' [84 *p. 278*], and many writers have seen this aim as the one thread of consistency that runs through all Disraeli's ideas and policies from first to last [104]. This was more than just the product of his romantic view of English history and society, as displayed in his early writings and novels [118]. For Disraeli, Robert Blake suggests, the 'aristocratic settlement' stood not only for that traditional order and stability – based on 'natural' leadership and rooted in common interests and mutual respect – that he saw epitomised in the rural society of his own county of Buckinghamshire, but for individual freedom [84 *pp. 278–82*]. These principles were the exact antithesis of what he conceived to be the typical evils of the age: Whig cosmopolitanism, the mercenary spirit of the manufacturing classes and the centralising tendencies of the Benthamite Radicals. Since these forces were the enemies also of the working classes, we have here the intellectual raw material of so-called 'Tory Democracy'. But to this traditional Conservatism based on 'the maintenance of our institutions' Disraeli added, in his great speech at the Crystal Palace in June 1872, two new principles:

'the preservation of our Empire and the improvement of the condition of the people', the latter point having already been developed in his famous *sanitas sanitatum* speech at Manchester a few months previously [*Doc. 9*].

It would, however, be an exaggeration as far as the first principle is concerned to imagine that Disraeli was here offering an ideology of imperialism to the Conservative Party, at least in the sense of support for a deliberate policy of colonial expansion and taking up 'the white man's burden'. Disraeli's imperialism was more limited, at once emotional and old-fashioned: it was not (as Shannon suggests) 'prophetic of a large new future' [13 *p. 106*]. He had no interest in colonial affairs as such, though he was fascinated by India and concerned for her security, as his Near Eastern policy and the proclamation of Queen Victoria as Empress of India in 1876 reveals. He was content to leave the details of local administration and policy to the men on the spot – disastrously as it turned out on the North-West Frontier of India and in South Africa. But he did have a vision of the Empire as a buttress to British military and foreign policy, 'a centralised military empire backing up the strength of Great Britain in her role as a world power and providing both resources and armies beyond the control of Parliament' [98 *pp. 180–1*]. This was a view which had already been adumbrated by Disraeli in speeches in 1866, and in action through the Abyssinian expedition of 1868. His purpose then, so it has been argued, was to stiffen the will to rule of the English upper classes, and at the same time, during these years of political crisis, damp down class conflicts by the pursuit of 'national' objectives [101].

Disraeli's second principle has been seized upon by Conservative apologists as well as historians and political writers, both then and since, who have argued that the Conservative Party under the inspiration of Disraeli adopted a clear consistent programme of social reform in order to win the support of the newly enfranchised working classes, and thus produce that union of the upper classes and the masses that would inaugurate 'Tory Democracy'. 'Disraeli discerned', in the famous comment of *The Times*, 'the Conservative workingman as the sculptor perceives the angel imprisoned in the block of marble' [167 *p. 11*].

But just as the traditional role of Disraeli in the Reform crisis of 1866–67 has come under heavy attack, so too has his role as a social reformer – notably by Professor Paul Smith [112]. What Paul Smith has shown by a detailed examination of the actual ideas and legislation of the Conservative Party in the field of social policy between 1866 and 1880 is how little of real substance there is in the popular view of Disraeli as an apostle of social reform. It is true that he did something to orientate his party in favour of 'the elevation of the condition of the People' in his speeches in 1872, partly at least to capture the working-class vote. But in practice all that Disraeli provided for his party were the verbal trappings of reform; after 1874 the choice of topics for legislative action and their detailed execution was left to middle-class outsiders such as R. A. Cross – 'the workhorse of the administration'. This was partly because Disraeli was over seventy when he achieved real power and, inevitably, lacked the energy of a Peel or a Gladstone; but it was also because, as Cross saw clearly but regretfully, Disraeli lacked that interest in, or grasp of, administrative detail so essential for the social reformer [*Doc. 10*]. Nevertheless, a more favourable view of Disraeli as a social reformer has been put forward by Peter Ghosh [100]. He suggests that it was Disraeli who provided the intellectual and emotional thrust for the Conservatives' legislation and ensured that it received the support of the Parliamentary Party. In this way, he believes, Disraeli helped to make social reform part of the tradition of the Conservative Party after 1880. Even so, such interest as Disraeli possessed in what a Conservative back-bencher called 'suet-pudding legislation', waned rapidly after 1876 in favour of ideas more in harmony with his flamboyant imagination: *imperium et libertas* instead of *sanitas sanitatum*. One historian has indeed commented on what he regards as 'the lack of purpose and creativity' in the Conservative government after that date [93 *p. 154*]; and this is symbolised perhaps by Disraeli's acceptance of a peerage in 1876 as the Earl of Beaconsfield, and his removal to the quieter pastures of the House of Lords.

Nor is it easy to see anything approaching a Conservative 'programme' of social reform during this period: indeed, there was nothing distinctly Conservative about the measures that were passed. 'Empiricism tempered by prejudice', in Paul Smith's phrase, remained the basis of the party's approach to social problems, and such problems were taken up and dealt with – or dropped – as and when political exigencies or public pressures demanded [112 *p. 200*]. Nevertheless, it would be unfair not to pay tribute to what was accomplished by Cross, Sandon and Sclater-Booth – with the backing of the Prime Minister – in the fields of education, housing, public health and labour legislation, in particular, during the three great years 1874 to 1876. In that period the Conservatives passed eleven major Acts. 'It was', concludes Smith, 'a considerable performance'; but, he adds, 'it was of rather mixed quality . . . if only the Licensing Act was a mistake, only the settlement of the labour laws was a triumph, and the remaining measures were cautious, limited, and even weak' [112 *p. 202*]. Why was this? The answer to that question tells us much about the Conservative Party and the pressures to which it was subject in the 1870s.

For though, as Disraeli and the more clear-headed members of the government realised, the Conservative Party had now to appeal more directly to the working-class electorate – and social reform could be conceived as one means towards that end – they could not afford to alienate their traditional supporters in the country or in the Commons. And the plain fact about the Conservative Party in the 1870s was that, despite the growing number of industrialists in its ranks and the appointment of a bookseller to the Cabinet, it was still primarily the party of the country gentry. Two hundred out of 350 Conservative MPs returned in 1874 were associated with the landed interest; and, unlike their Liberal opposite numbers, they were largely unrestrained by any systematic outside pressure from, for example, organisations like the National Education League. It was their ethos therefore that dominated the party, and, inevitably, the country gentry were often unsympathetic to the new tensions and problems that faced the party leadership. What often inhibited a bold Conservative social policy, therefore, were the ineluctable pressures of prejudice and vested interest within the party: suspicion of centralisation, devotion to the dogmas of *laissez-faire* and, above all, blind opposition to anything – votes for labourers, higher rates, elected school boards, trade unions – that would upset the established order in the English shires. Even the reformers largely accepted these presuppositions. Lord Sandon's purpose in his Education Act of 1876 was, *inter alia*, to free the countryside from school boards – as he said, 'the favourite platforms of the Dissenting preacher and the local agitator' [112 *p. 246*]. In the end, therefore, it was only the mildness and limited nature of the government's social reforms that made them palatable to the country gentry.

But there was another, more profound, reason for the limitations of Conservative social policy. For the Second Reform Act had a paradoxical effect. If, on the one hand, it created a mass working-class electorate that could be won for the Conservative Party, it also helped, by its invocation of democracy, to create those fears and apprehensions among the middle classes that would slowly drive them away from the Liberal Party. After 1867 the Conservative Party became increasingly attractive to an urban bourgeoisie whose members were more and more appalled by Gladstonian 'energy' and the rise of the working class in social and political power; and the Conservative leadership was bound to attune its policy accordingly. 'We came in', said Disraeli after the 1874 election, 'on the principle of not harassing the country' [6 *p. 85*] The Conservatives were compelled, therefore, during this period to appeal more and more to the middle, rather than the working, class, especially as they needed their support as leaders in the new borough Conservative Associations. This meant that though social legislation could be used to win over the workers, it must not be so radical as to frighten away the middle class; its distinctly 'class' nature must be toned down. Nor was it only middle-class voters that Disraeli had to worry about: the great forces of industrial and commercial wealth – rapidly coalescing with the older landed interest in the Conservative Party – had also to be conciliated. It is this that helps to explain why the government was so often willing to yield – unless browbeaten by the righteous wrath of a Samuel Plimsoll – to the vested interests of mineowners, brewers and shipowners.

Here we have the dilemma of the Conservative Party in the 1870s and indeed later. How could it provide policies which would appeal to the working classes without frightening away the middle classes? The answer provided by Disraeli after 1876 was to stress 'national' rather than 'class' policies; policies that highlighted not the special class interests of the workers, but rather what they had in common with the rest of the community. As he said, in a famous comment, 'I have always considered that the Tory party was the national party of England' [84 *p. 482*]. This meant an emphasis on the mutual interests of the working classes and the classes above them, led by their 'natural' leaders in the Conservative Party, in supporting the country's institutions – Monarchy, Church, Aristocracy – as outlined in the Prime Minister's earlier speeches.

It also meant, more importantly, a deliberate return to Palmerstonian policies after a period when, according to Disraeli, the Liberals had pursued a policy of appeasement in foreign affairs and aimed at 'the disintegration of the Empire of England' [110 *p. 98*]. This involved a vigorous assertion of British power abroad and particularly the defence of national interests in the Indian Empire and the eastern Mediterranean, both of which seemed threatened by Russian expansion in the 1870s. This policy can be seen in Disraeli's much-publicised coup in 1875 – the purchase of the Suez Canal shares, which gave Britain a stake in the control of this important new sea route to India [98]. It was also exemplified by his belligerent attitude towards Russia in defence of the integrity of the Turkish Empire. Unfortunately, this commitment meant that Disraeli was forced to play down the effects of Turkish repression against their Christian subjects in the Balkans, who were demanding independence, and especially the extent of the Turkish massacres of the Bulgarian rebels in 1875–76. The horror aroused by the massacres in Great Britain led to a great national campaign – the Bulgarian Agitation of 1876 – organised mainly by Radicals and nonconformists and directed against the government's eastern policy. The publication of Gladstone's notorious pamphlet, *The Bulgarian Horrors*, in September, provided 'a unifying text and a charismatic leader' [110 *p. 282*], and made him the dominating figure in the agitation. This marks the re-entry of the great Liberal statesman into active politics after his retirement from the Liberal leadership in the previous year. Gladstone demanded that the Turks leave the Balkans 'bag and baggage'; and he believed that the creation of self-governing states in the Balkans was not only morally right, but would provide a more effective barrier to Russian domination than propping up the decrepit Turkish Empire [73].

For the moment, however, Disraeli's eastern policy commanded wide support. The outbreak of war between Russia and Turkey in 1877 and the advance of Russia towards Constantinople, led to a great outbreak of 'Jingoism' in England and demands for war against the aggressor, a mood to which Disraeli responded by actively organising military and naval preparations against Russia and threatening war. One result of the Prime Minister's bellicose stance, however, was the resignation of his pacific Foreign Secretary, Lord Derby, together with Lord Carnarvon, the Colonial Secretary. Derby was replaced by Lord Salisbury, an outstanding appointment as it turned out. But these resignations marked the first real break in the unity of the Disraeli Administration. War between Great Britain and Russia was narrowly averted when Russia agreed to attend a congress of the Great Powers at Berlin in 1878 to work out a settlement of the problems of the Near East. This led eventually to the signing of the Treaty of Berlin in July 1878. Disraeli then returned to England, bringing with him (in his own famous phrase) 'peace with honour'. This was a great personal triumph. The Prime Minister could claim that Russian power in the Balkans had been reduced by forcing her to agree to abandon her support for a 'Big Bulgaria' under Russian influence, and the Turkish Empire had therefore been given a new lease of life. In addition, in order to strengthen British power in the eastern Mediterranean, Turkey had yielded Cyprus to Great Britain in return for a new defensive alliance.

The forceful assertion of British interests abroad was also reflected in the government's 'forward' policies in Afghanistan and South Africa in 1879, though these at least were initiated by the men on the spot, Lord Lytton, the Viceroy of India, and Sir Bartle Frere, High Commissioner at the Cape of Good Hope.

It cannot be said that Disraeli's attempt to 'wrap the Tories in the Union Jack' (in Vincent's phrase) paid high dividends for his party, or at least not immediately [118 *p. 15*]. Both the Afghan and Zulu wars were punctuated by early military disasters, and though the British army later won significant victories, no permanent solutions to the imperial problems involved in both areas were obtained by the time the Conservatives left office in 1880. The 'little wars' in Afghanistan and South Africa were also expensive. They forced Lord Northcote, the Chancellor of the Exchequer, to raise income tax, something which was bound to add to the unpopularity of the government during the period of economic depression which hit the country at the end of the 1870s. Nor was the government's eastern policy any more successful in the long run. As Lord Salisbury himself pointed out after the Congress of Berlin: 'I think we have got as good a settlement as could fairly be expected – without bloodshed. But we have not settled the Eastern Question' [116 *pp. 101–2*]. Even the acquisition of Cyprus became redundant after the occupation of Egypt in the 1880s. Moreover, nearer home and more immediately, Gladstone seized with both hands the opportunity to denounce the 'immorality' of Disraeli's whole foreign and imperial policy in his Midlothian Campaign of 1879–80. Disraeli's political strategy of winning over public opinion by a brilliant display abroad collapsed in ruins at the general election of 1880.

In that election the Conservative Party lost more than 100 seats, and all the gains made in 1874 were wiped out. They lost most heavily in the large boroughs where, out of 114 seats, they now had only twenty-four; though, on the other hand, they did well in the City of London and London suburbia. They also lost twenty-seven county seats, and were practically wiped out in Wales and Scotland. In the end, the Liberals gained an overall majority of about fifty, and the swing to them would probably have been even stronger if the large number of uncontested seats had been fought. The Conservative Party seemed, therefore, to be back to where it was in 1868. 'The downfall of Beaconsfieldism', said Gladstone, 'is like the vanishing of some vast magnificent castle in an Italian romance' [66, ii, *p. 223*]. The Conservatives therefore faced the grim prospect that their period of power between 1874 and 1880 was merely a temporary interlude in the onward march of Liberalism which had proceeded since 1830 [69]. Curiously, Disraeli himself was never more popular than in this hour of defeat. Supported after his resignation as Prime Minister by a unanimous and enthusiastic vote of confidence, he decided to carry on as party leader, determined to act, as he said in a letter to Lord Lytton, 'as if I were still young and vigorous, and take all steps in my power to sustain the spirit and restore the discipline of the Tory Party' [84, *p. 721*]. With this typically jaunty courage the old statesman carried on for another year until his death in April 1881.

Why then did the Conservatives lose the general election of 1880 [142]? There were, in the first place, a number of electoral factors which put the Liberals in a stronger position from the start. The timing of the election (as with Gladstone in 1874) was unexpected and unfavourable to the Conservatives, since Disraeli delayed until the euphoria that followed the Treaty of Berlin had largely passed away. No real reply was made by Disraeli to the attack on 'Beaconsfieldism' proclaimed so passionately by Gladstone in the Midlothian Campaign, and in any case the major Conservative spokesmen during the campaign – owing to the convention by which peers did not participate – were easily outgunned by the Liberals [Doc. 11]. Furthermore, the Conservative Party machine had been allowed to run down, especially after the resignation in 1877 of J. A. Gorst, its real creator and the one true Tory Democrat in the party [133 *ch. 6*]. Nor, surprisingly, did the Conservatives make much of their record in social reform during the campaign – another indication perhaps of its limited role. Clearly, it was not considered a trump card as far as the working-class voter was concerned, or at least not effective enough to offset the more immediate impact of industrial depression.

It is in fact the depression that has generally been regarded as the major factor in causing the Conservative defeat. Disraeli himself said: 'Hard Times, as far as I can [re]collect, has been our foe, and certainly the alleged cause of our downfall' [84 *p. 719*]. Most of his colleagues agreed. And the effects of depression were unmistakable. Some businesses faced bankruptcy and ruin. Real wages fell by 5 per cent during 1873–79; the average level of unemployment (as revealed by trade union statistics) rose from 1 or 2 per cent in 1871–74 to about 11 per cent in 1879, a year of real distress among sections of the working class. For the farmers, too, 1879 was a bad year. All that the government did for them, however – apart from one unsatisfactory Act to provide compensation for improvements – was to appoint the Richmond Commission to investigate the causes of agricultural depression. It was this negative attitude that led to the growth of the Farmers' Alliance, an independent farmers' movement which put up its own candidates at the election and thus helped to produce the slump in Tory votes in the counties [135]. The agricultural depression was particularly bad in Ireland, whose affairs had been almost completely neglected by Disraeli, and this led to the beginnings of the Land War between landlords and tenants and encouraged the expansion of the Home Rule Party.

Of course, as Disraeli insisted, the coming of depression was bad luck for the Conservative Party, since it could not reasonably be regarded as directly responsible for its onset. But it was undoubtedly true that the government did little to cope with its consequences. Indeed, how could it? It had no more notion of what to do than its opponents or its successors in the 1920s, apart from the suggestion of setting up a Relief Committee to cope with the distress among the working classes. In this situation Disraeli was completely at sea. 'And yet – what is the cause of the distress?', he wrote plaintively to a friend. 'And if permanent, is there to be a permanent Committee of Relief. . . . You must see . . . how difficult is my present position with constant correspondence . . . of equal and contradictory character . . . everybody agreeing with nobody but throwing the responsibility on my shoulders' [110 *p. 338*]. Neither Disraeli nor his colleagues believed that there was much that could be done. Protection was ruled out as a cure for the country's economic ills on political grounds – it would be electoral suicide. The only thing to do, therefore, as W. H. Smith suggested, was, resignedly, to await the return of better times. The Conservatives, however, not unfairly, were bound to be blamed by the country for the effects of the depression; just as Disraeli was castigated by Gladstone for the iniquitous results of his foreign and imperial policies.

The election of 1880 does much to illuminate the nature of Disraelian Conservatism. It is true, of course, that the Conservative Party, mainly under Disraeli's inspiration, did make a real attempt to enlarge the electoral basis of its strength, and thus provided, in Paul Smith's words, 'a classic case of successful adaptation to a changing environment' [112 *pp. 1–2*]. This is indicated, to some extent, by the fact that, despite losing two elections, the

Conservatives were increasing their votes in industrial seats during the whole period 1868–80; and even in 1880 their proportion of the poll rose by 7 per cent in large constituencies. But, as we have already seen, the social policy of the Conservatives was not really well adapted to the purpose of winning over the working-class voters; electorally, as the verdict of 1880 seemed to show, it was almost irrelevant, and seems to have done little to wean the workers away from the Liberal Party. Indeed, the government's trade union legislation – by restoring the right of peaceful picketing – helped to heal the one great breach between organised labour and official Liberalism, and therefore probably precipitated the return of the trade union voter to the Liberal Party. The policy of the Conservative Party, said Disraeli after his resignation in 1880, 'is to maintain the Empire and preserve the Constitution' [84 *p. 721*]. Social reform was now conspicuous by its absence from the great triumvirate of Conservative aims that he had formerly proclaimed in 1872; and indeed imperialism and the preservation of the *status quo* were to be the Disraelian themes that emerged most distinctly in the Conservative Party of the later nineteenth century.

Disraeli's political reputation has, on the whole, received a rough handling from present-day historians. Though they acknowledge his success in restoring Conservative fortunes after 1867, his role as a supporter of democracy and as a committed social reformer has been challenged (as we saw earlier) by historians such as Maurice Cowling, E. J. Feuchtwanger and Paul Smith [17; 133; 112]. Recent writers are even more sceptical about Disraeli's practical achievements as a statesman, and particularly the claim that he 'educated' his party. Coleman suggests that 'he did little to reshape Conservatism significantly in either thought or policy' [93 *p. 157*]. 'The most consistent strain in Disraeli's career', writes Ian Machin, 'was his determination to gain and keep political power' [105 *p. 5*]; his policies, suggests another historian, 'were mainly a matter of style and presentation' [119 *p. 47*]; while the best that John Vincent can say in favour of Disraeli the politician is that he was 'the greatest leader of the opposition modern Britain has known' [118 *p. 6*].

Why then, given this apparent lack of solid achievement, is Disraeli still regarded as an outstanding figure in the history of the modern Conservative Party? Some historians believe that this was due primarily to the posthumous reputation built up for him by apologists and party propagandists in the years after his death in 1881 [110; iii; 118]. For what the Conservative Party needed in the age of mass politics and the popular Press that developed in the later years of the nineteenth century, was a cult – an image – to stir and impress the voters, at a time when they had no outstanding leaders who appealed to the popular imagination. For Conservatives, Disraeli fitted the bill perfectly. He was an extraordinary personality of distinctive appearance, a courageous fighter from an unprivileged background, a master of wit and epigram, and a figure of warmth and optimism. All this, when combined with a suitably touched-up portrait of his political career, meant that Disraeli could easily be turned into an exponent of 'Tory Democracy', or, later, in the twentieth century, of 'One-Nation Toryism'.

PART TWO: THE STRUGGLE

3 PARTY ORGANISATION

Political parties, if they are to win elections, require not only policies but organisation. Before 1867, however, with a small electorate the problem was not so urgent, and party organisation was primitive, makeshift and erratic, springing into life only when a general election was pending. The central organisation of the parties in the 1860s was normally in the hands of the Whips, whose main task, apart from their parliamentary duties, was to raise money for the election fund and obtain candidates, functions they normally performed under the benevolent but aloof authority of the party leader. The only practical help the Whips obtained was from the services, part-time and generally unofficial, of an election or party agent, together with the help of an occasional interested party notable. Nationally, in the counties and boroughs, party affairs were in the hands of virtually self-appointed and self-perpetuating committees of local party bigwigs, who ran the constituency with the help of a registration agent for day-to-day business and advice and, at election times, a paid election agent [Doc. 12]. The links between the central and local party organisers were inevitably very tenuous, and were conducted mainly through the great London political clubs: the Carlton (Conservative) founded in 1832, and the Reform (Liberal) 1836.

The Second Reform Act of 1867 had a decisive effect on the development of party organisation. Both parties now had to win the votes of a much wider – mainly working-class – electorate, especially in the large boroughs; and the new and often taxing problems that this posed for the party managers can be seen exemplified in the correspondence of Glyn and Brand, the Liberal Whips, at the election of 1868. 'The old lines of a general election do not serve us now', Glyn wrote to Gladstone, 'all is new and changed and . . . I fear I must say in some respects dark' [153 p. 189]. The period between 1867 and 1886 was essentially a transitional period in party organisation. New and more efficient machinery was created to cope with the problems of a mass electorate, and active party membership began to become a reality; but all this existed side by side with the antediluvian methods and ideas of a bygone political age. Two major developments in fact took place. First, organisation at the centre became more professional and more formalised, and both Conservatives and Liberals established a central party office in London [*Doc. 13*]. Secondly, local party organisations were set up throughout the country, concentrated mainly in the large boroughs, and these eventually coalesced to form national organisations – the Conservative National Union (1867) and the National Liberal Federation (1877). Linked with these were their fellow-travelling organisations and pressure groups: the powerful Liberal Liberation Society, for example, and, in the 1880s, the tamer Conservative Primrose, and Fair Trade, Leagues.

The two great national organisations, however, though of major importance as propaganda and 'ginger' groups for the Conservative and Liberal Parties, did pose a frightening problem for the party leaders: might they not use their broad-based power to dictate to the parliamentary parties? Thus the problem of the relationship between the parliamentary parties, on the one hand, and the Conservative National Union and Liberal Federation, on the other, proved to be one of the great themes in the history of party organisation in the later nineteenth century. But the fear of 'caucus control' – dictation to Parliament by outside irresponsible bodies – which so worried political commentators in the 1870s and 1880s, and was later given classic expression in Ostrogorski's great book, proved in the end to be an illusion [148]. By the turn of the century the leaders of both parties had, in McKenzie's phrase, 'shackled the monster they had created', and the pattern of party organisation then established persisted, with minor modifications, well into the twentieth century [146 *p. 9*].

THE CONSERVATIVE PARTY

For the Conservative Party, lacking those unofficial lines of communication between party and people which were established by the Liberals in the 1860s, efficient national organisation was an absolute necessity. But just as the problems of Conservative 'policy' after the passing of the Second Reform Act had aroused tensions and conflicts within the party, so too did the problems of organisation. Should it be 'popular' organisation, appealing directly to and involving the middle and working classes; or should it be 'authoritarian', directed from above by the traditional hierarchy of party leader, aristocratic Whips and part-time aides? The conflict between these two conceptions had arisen as early as 1867 at the formation of the Conservative National Union. It soon affected Disraeli's first major step in improving central party organisation – the establishment of the Conservative Central Office in 1870 and the appointment of J. A. Gorst as party agent.

Gorst, a clear-headed and vigorous administrator, aimed primarily at improving Conservative organisation in the large boroughs, which meant appealing directly to the working class. During the next few years he was extraordinarily successful. By the end of 1873 Gorst was able to report to Disraeli that sixty-nine new Conservative Associations had been founded, and that more than 400 Associations were in existence throughout the country, including thirty-three in the forty-nine largest boroughs. It was here, in the larger boroughs, that the influence of the Central Office was strongest; the smaller boroughs and, even more, the counties, were willy-nilly allowed to go their own way. By the time of the general election in 1874 a Conservative candidate had been found for every reasonable constituency, and Gorst's efforts seemed to be rewarded by the Conservative victory at the polls [133 *ch. 5*].

The other significant development in Conservative Party organisation during this period was the foundation of the National Union in 1867. Here too the initiative came, not, as with the National Liberal Federation, from below, but from above. 'The National Union was organised', said Henry Raikes, one of its founders, 'rather as a handmaid to the party, than to usurp the functions of party leadership' [126 *p. 259*]. The inaugural meeting of the Union on 12 November 1867 assembled sixty-seven delegates from fifty-five cities: Gorst took the chair in the absence of a peer! But despite the Union's ostensible aim of winning over the working class, the emphasis in electing officers was on 'men of influence and prestige', not working men, an illuminating illustration of the ambivalent attitude of the Conservative Party in the post-Reform epoch. Indeed, though the Union did good work in issuing pamphlets etc., by the election of 1868 it was practically moribund as an independent organisation – a clear reflection of its lack of consistent purpose and the absence of outstanding party leaders from its councils. When, in 1871, Gorst became its Secretary and transferred its headquarters to his own offices as party agent in Parliament Street, the National Union became in practice what it had always really been in theory, the propaganda arm of the Conservative Central Office.

The foundation of the National Union in 1867 and the Central Office in 1870 were, as Feuchtwanger says, 'the most important permanent legacy of the period' [133 *p. xiii*]. But they produced no fundamental change in the structure of the party, and were largely ignored or opposed by the traditionalists. Hence the same old battles were fought after 1874 as before. For, foolishly, the party leaders not only allowed the machine which had been carefully built up in the previous four years to run down, but encouraged the central control of the party organisation to pass from Gorst (whose engagement as party agent officially ended in 1874) back to the Whips – the representatives of the aristocratic element in the party. Gorst, who had in any case become a member of Parliament in 1875 and was anxious to carve out a political career for himself, resigned in disgust in 1877 after warning Disraeli of the dangers now facing the party [133 *pp. 137–8*], though Disraeli himself, significantly, had acquiesced in this shift to the right in the party. Panic-stricken by the electoral disaster of 1880, the party managers hastily turned back to Gorst who was re-engaged as party agent, and a new permanent Central Committee, ostensibly representing all sections of the party, was set up to supervise organisation [*Doc. 14*]. Yet the old antagonisms between the cantankerous party agent and the party managers soon cropped up again. Outwardly, these concerned control of finance, demarcation of responsibility, and similar problems; but Gorst saw them, more fundamentally, as an attempt by the Conservative 'old gang' to re-establish control, a claim which was given additional weight by the similar unhappy experience of his successor, G. C. T. Bartley, who became party agent in 1882 [*Doc. 15*]. Disillusioned, Bartley too resigned – as did Winn, the Chief Whip – in 1885. Their replacement by Captain Middleton as party agent and Akers-Douglas as Chief Whip, together with the fact that the electoral legislation of 1883–85 had revolutionised the conditions of political life, began something of a new era in the central organisation of the Conservative Party [146].

Before this could be achieved, one final problem had to be settled: the revival of the National Union under the dynamic leadership of Lord Randolph Churchill. Since 1880 Lord Randolph had built up a brilliant reputation as leader of the 'Fourth Party' in the House of Commons – a minuscule group which consisted, apart from himself, of his friends J. A. Gorst, Drummond Wolff and A. J. Balfour [103 *ch. 3*] Churchill's main task, and one which he carried out with extraordinary skill and panache, was to harass and hold up to ridicule the Liberal government in the House of Commons, and especially its aged leader, particularly over Ireland and 'the Bradlaugh Case'. In the latter affair, Gladstone supported the claim of the notorious atheist, Charles Bradlaugh – thrice elected MP for Northampton – to take his seat in the House of Commons. Churchill's subsidiary aim was to attack the pusillanimous spirit displayed by his own leader in the House, Sir Stafford Northcote, and the absurd arrangement by which, since Disraeli's death in 1881, he had shared power with Lord Salisbury in the Upper House. In many ways, therefore, as his support for the independent leadership of Lord Salisbury indicates, Lord Randolph was advocating a more pugnacious brand of traditional Toryism, rather than 'Tory Democracy', the name with which his ideas are usually branded [109]; though (as Foster suggests) he offered no clear consistent view of what he meant by 'Toryism' [99]. What really moved Churchill in the early 1880s was not policy, which meant little to him, but, as both his recent biographers agree, personal ambition and, it must be said, delight in the battle for its own sake [99; 103]. What he wanted to do after 1882 was to lever himself into the front rank of the Conservative Party by sheer effrontery and oratorical brilliance; and in the National Union the instrument for his purposes lay at hand. He set out, therefore, to capture it.

The National Union in 1883 was in many ways admirably adapted for Churchill's plans. It had in the 1870s quietly toed the central party line; but now, with nearly 500 Associations affiliated to it, it could be said to represent the real voice of the Conservative Party, and many ordinary Conservatives, appalled by the electoral disaster of 1880, and impressed by the evident success of the National Liberal Federation, were intensely worried by the weaknesses of official Conservatism, and were crying out for full-blooded leadership. It was their hopes and fears that Churchill used, and became spokesman for. Moreover, the unwieldy constitution of the Union could easily be manipulated by a determined 'caucus' of Lord Randolph and his friends; and here the support of Gorst, with his mastery of party organisation, was absolutely priceless. In 1883 the young aristocratic crusader made his bid to capture the Union. He was not completely successful, but he did well enough to become Chairman and obtain a small but decisive 'Churchillian' majority on the Council. He then threw down his challenge to Northcote and Salisbury by demanding that real power be given to the National Union; that, in the words of the

1883 Conference resolution, the Union 'secure its legitimate influence in the party organisation' [87 *p. 203*]. Another weapon used by Lord Randolph against the party leadership was the Primrose League, which he and his friends and allies founded in November 1883, ostensibly in memory of Disraeli. It was intended to be an unofficial, popular political organisation, appealing to all classes at grass-roots level, and spreading the gospel of Toryism. 'It provided a raucous but effective vehicle of propaganda for Churchill as much as for Toryism' [99 *p. 132*]. Thus began that behind-the-scenes struggle between Lord Randolph Churchill and Lord Salisbury which posed yet again the fundamental problem: should the Conservative Party be a 'popular' or an 'authoritarian' organisation? A long period of conflict, negotiation, recrimination and misunderstanding now followed, in which Lord Randolph resigned as Chairman, was reinstated in triumph at the Sheffield Conference of the National Union in July 1884, but then unexpectedly came to terms with Lord Salisbury. This new-found Conservative unity was hastened by the possibility of the Liberal government's immediate collapse and an early general election. By their agreement, Lord Randolph recognised Lord Salisbury as party leader and entered the fold himself as a member of the upper party hierarchy; he resigned as Chairman of the National Union and was replaced by Michael Hicks-Beach. On the other hand, the old Central Committee was dissolved and Lord Salisbury officially recognised the Primrose League.

This was really a victory for Lord Salisbury and the official leadership of the Conservative Party. For whereas Lord Randolph regarded the National Union merely as a ladder for his ambition, which, once used, could easily be discarded, both Salisbury and Northcote were adamant in their refusal to give up their essential control of the party, and, given their firmness, Churchill was bound to lose. He stood for no new ideas or principles, no new social or economic group in the politics of the 1880s; the alternative Churchill presented to the Conservative Party was, as Salisbury probably realised, a sham alternative [99; 102; 109]. In any case, it was not new ideas that the Conservative Party was hankering after during this period, nor were the rank and file in the National Union really protesting against central leadership as such; it was weak leadership they objected to, and Lord Salisbury was soon to give them the strong and effective leadership they demanded. It was, therefore, the anguish of defeat, and not any fundamental change in party ethos, that gave Lord Randolph his brief period of success as a 'popular' politician. As for the National Union, it was, in Sir Winston Churchill's phrase, 'peacefully laid to rest' by Michael Hicks-Beach [92 *p. 359*]. Unhappily for Lord Randolph, by throwing away the prop which had brought him to power, he placed himself at the mercy of his former rivals, and thus prepared the way for his later dramatic downfall [138].

THE LIBERAL PARTY

Like the Conservatives, the Liberals also established a Central (Registration) Association during this period, but on the whole, partly due to the nature of the Liberal Party, partly due to the lack of anyone like Gorst, it was controlled almost completely by the Whips. Brand and Glyn, Chief Whips between 1857 and 1873, did good work in building up contact between the central organisation and the local Liberal Associations in the immediate post-Reform period. But the fact that there was no great change in either the machinery or the personnel of the Liberal Central Office was relatively unimportant, since the real changes in party organisation came not from above but from below: it was the changes at the grass roots that were of major importance. Here – as with the campaign for secular education – Birmingham again provided the driving force and example by developing a new and, as some thought, sinister form of organisation – the Caucus.

The Birmingham Liberal Association had been founded in 1865, and from the start differed from the older type of oligarchic association by being open to anyone in the city. It was soon remodelled by its secretary, William Harris, on a popular but strongly centralised basis, ranging from the elected ward committee at the bottom, through the Central Committee of 600, which nominated parliamentary candidates, to the Central Executive, and the 'Council of Ten' at the top, the brains and will of the whole organisation. In origin, however, the Caucus, as it was dubbed by Disraeli – in a word drawn from American politics – was neither as original, nor as much the result of malevolent calculation as Ostrogorski made out in his classical study [148]. What was new about the Caucus of 1867 was not so much its underlying ideas or its methods – since the working class and the middle class in Birmingham had been co-operating mutually in reform politics since the 1830s – but the formalisation of its machinery and its adaptation to an enlarged electorate, an electorate which accepted, naturally, the tutelage of the middle class. Indeed, as T. R. Tholfsen argues convincingly, the Caucus was related directly to the ethos of the Birmingham community, and emerged slowly and naturally out of the rich soil of its economic, social and religious life [152]. The effectiveness of this new organisation was seen when all three Liberals were returned at the election of 1868 despite the fact that the Second Reform Act had given each elector only two votes; and – especially owing to the work of Francis Schnadhorst who succeeded William Harris in 1873 – the Liberals easily won the school board and council elections in the same year. As a result Joseph Chamberlain became Mayor of Birmingham in 1873, and began his great programme of civic improvement which, over the next three years, helped to make the city – in his own proud boast – 'the best governed city in the world' [1 *p. 89*]. In 1874 the Association's three candidates were returned unopposed at the general election [145]. The Liberal Party was now supreme in Birmingham, sustained by the power of radical nonconformity.

The defeat of 1874 gave a considerable stimulus to the establishment of 'popular' Liberal Associations in many other great cities, such as Leeds, Sheffield, Bradford, Newcastle; and though they differed from the Birmingham Association in particulars, the Birmingham Radicals, as Professor Hanham says, 'supplied the associations with both an ideology and an organisational model' [135 *p. 133*]. As yet, however, there was no unified organisation or policy for them all: this Joseph Chamberlain and his Radical associates set out to provide. By the mid 1870s in fact Chamberlain was tiring of the education issue alone as a spearhead of radical attack since it failed to arouse any great enthusiasm in the country at large. 'I don't think the League will do', he told Dilke in 1873 when he was already thinking in terms of a reconstructed Liberal Party with a wide reform programme and new leaders [30]. The electoral disaster of 1874 confirmed Chamberlain's gloomy forebodings about the future of the Liberal Party. His return, unopposed, as one of the members for Birmingham in 1876, by which time Lord Hartington had succeeded Gladstone as Liberal leader, only underlined his disillusionment with official Liberalism. When, therefore, in the same year William Harris proposed to Chamberlain a national radical organisation linking all the 'pressure' groups – National Education League, Liberation Society etc. – and based on the Liberal Associations, he took up the idea enthusiastically, insisting only that it be based on Birmingham, and notices were sent to all associations organised on a 'popular' basis to send delegates to a national conference to be held at Birmingham on 31 May 1877.

The year 1876 was important, however, for another reason. It was the year when Gladstone re-emerged from retirement to become one of the leaders of the Bulgarian Agitation directed against Disraeli's Eastern policy. The Agitation – strongly supported by Radicals and nonconformists – thus provided the background, though not as Ostrogorski believed the original stimulus, for the foundation of the National Liberal Federation. That was provided by the National Education League which, after it was wound up in the spring of 1877, bequeathed its pattern of organisation, its sectarian passion and much of its personnel to the new organisation [137].

We are just going to issue the League's dissolution circular [wrote Chamberlain to John Morley in February 1877], announcing at the same time the formation of a Federation of Liberal Associations with hq at Birmingham and the League Officers as chief cooks. I think this may become a very powerful organisation and proportionately detested by all Whips and Whigs. [41, i *p. 258*]

The inaugural meeting took place at Birmingham as planned. There, with Chamberlain acting as President and his henchman, Jesse Collings, as Secretary, a constitution and statement of policy was drawn up for the new National Liberal Federation. The meeting was not a complete success. Only about half of the hundred or so delegates agreed to join, owing to fears for their local autonomy, and of the pressure groups, only the National Education League, as we have seen, agreed to commit suicide to please Mr Chamberlain. The Federation, however, held its first meeting at Birmingham on 22 July 1877. Joseph Chamberlain was elected President; William Harris, Chairman; Jesse Collings, Hon. Secretary, and Francis Schnadhorst, paid Secretary; three subcommittees were set up and a central office in Birmingham [*Doc. 18*]. By 1879 the new Secretary's organising genius had brought in over 100 Liberal Associations, though nearly all were in the provinces and hardly any in London.

It was the formation of the National Liberal Federation that really sparked off the grand debate on the merits and defects of the Caucus. For Joseph Chamberlain and his friends, the Caucus meant a 'democratisation' of the Liberal Party by, as he wrote, 'the direct participation of all its members in the direction of its policy and in the selection of those particular measures of reform to which priority shall be given' [129 *p. 133*]. Such a conception of party organisation implied an attack on the domination of the Whigs within the party, as reflected in both the leadership and the Whips' Office, and a demand for renewed energy, enthusiasm and purpose within contemporary Liberalism [*Doc. 19*]. It was this emphasis on 'action' that appealed to Gladstone, and that led him – obsessed as he was with the Eastern Question – to give the Federation his political blessing by addressing its inaugural meeting in May 1877. Equally typically, Lord Granville warned him against going, and Lord Hartington refused to recognise the Federation at all [*Doc. 20*].

If these arch-Whigs damned the Caucus with faint praise, other critics were more forthright in their denunciations. It was argued that the Caucus organisation gave power to a ruthless (and probably corrupt) faction, who not only manipulated the whole Federation in the interests of Birmingham, but through their control of voters, parliamentary candidates and policy would eventually dictate to Parliament itself. Probably the truth is, as Professor Hanham suggests, somewhere between the two extremes [135 ch. 7]. Certainly, Chamberlain's more extravagant claims on behalf of the 'democracy' of the Caucus were patently absurd, since in practice, if not in theory, power fell more and more into the hands of the Executive Committee, and the Associations soon came to represent no one but themselves. 'The popular form of the party Organisation', in Ostrogorski's harsh judgement, 'merely enables the latter to penetrate deeper into the masses for the purpose of capturing them more easily, and not for giving them independence' [148 *p. 303*].

The machinery of the Caucus did seem to be justified by the Liberal victory in 1880, when Chamberlain and Schnadhorst claimed that the Liberals gained or retained sixty out of sixty-seven constituencies where 'popular' associations existed. The claim was somewhat exaggerated [145], but even opponents such as Disraeli and Churchill were impressed. This flush of success, increased by Chamberlain's appointment to the Cabinet in 1880, and the rise in the number of affiliated associations in the 1880s, did lead to the Federation asserting itself more forcefully. If it did not yet formulate a party programme and try to impose it on the party leadership, it at least claimed the right to ascertain and express specific policies, such as franchise reform, in accordance with its Conference resolution in 1881. 'A mere telegram from the bigwigs of the

Caucus,' wrote Ostrogorski with typical exaggeration, 'was enough to set the Associations in motion throughout the country, and the lion growled, screamed, moved with pleasure or with anger as occasion required' [148 *pp. 209–10*].

The beast was soon to be tamed. In 1884 Schnadhorst resigned as Secretary of the Birmingham Liberal Association to become full-time Secretary of the National Liberal Federation; and owing to the influence of Joseph Chamberlain, who was anxious to curb Whig influence at the centre, he was also given a seat on the Standing Committee of the Liberal Central Office – a poacher turned gamekeeper. Two years later, in 1886, he became Secretary of the Central Office also, and the National Liberal Federation's headquarters were moved from Birmingham to join it in London. In this way Schnadhorst was able to control the Liberal organisation both nationally and at the centre. But by that time, owing to the split in the party over Home Rule, it was to be used not to increase but to destroy the power of his former master, Joseph Chamberlain [145]. A new phase in the history of the Liberal Party and the National Liberal Federation began in 1886.

THE LATER NINETEENTH CENTURY

The most important influence on political practice in the later nineteenth century was the great trio of laws passed by the Liberals in the 1880s: the Corrupt and Illegal Practices Act of 1883, the Third Reform Act of 1884 and the Redistribution Act of 1885. By effectively limiting election expenses, the first Act 'transformed the whole character of British electioneering within a generation' [147 *p. 175*]. It did this in two ways. In the long run it meant that poorer men could become parliamentary candidates; more immediately, it made voluntary work at elections more and more vital, and therefore emphasised the importance of party membership in the constituencies. It is in this way that the Primrose League came into its own. After its official recognition by Lord Salisbury in 1884, it became the most important arm of the Conservative Party at grass-roots level. For, despite its rather absurd pseudo-medieval structure, which replicated the existing class system, and its quaint rituals, emblems, and titles, the Primrose League was a shrewd and effective political organisation. In particular, its recruitment of, and involvement of, women in day-to-day political activity at local level – at a time when they did not possess the vote – and its emphasis on entertainments and social activities as the mainstay of Conservative propaganda and recruitment, gave it an enormous appeal, particularly to the middle classes. Nor was any of this a threat to the party leadership. In its propaganda, the Primrose League concentrated on the great commonplaces of Tory belief – Religion, Monarchy, Empire – and did not concern itself with contemporary problems or party policy. The League really took off during the general elections of 1885 and 1886; by 1887 it had half-a-million members, and by the end of the century, one-and-a-half million. It thus became 'the largest and most widely spread political organisation of the time' [108 *p. 28*].

The two Reform Acts of 1884 and 1885 also had an important effect on party organisation. For the equalising of the franchise in boroughs and counties and the introduction of single-member constituencies throughout much of the country meant, as Ensor suggests, that 'the individual for the first time became the unit and numerical equality . . . the master principle' [5 *p. 88*]. This was not in fact entirely true in detail [127]. Nevertheless, the increase in the unity and standardisation of the electoral system, accompanied as it was by the rise of national leaders and national issues in the later years of the nineteenth century, was bound to enlarge also the influence of the party Central Offices. And this fitted in with tendencies operating within the parties themselves.

In the Conservative Party, the end of Lord Randolph Churchill's *mésalliance* with the National Union was followed by its reorganisation, on paper at least. In 1885 every Conservative Association was automatically affiliated to the National Union, and it thus became a really national organisation; in the following year ten Provincial Unions were established. It is true that these reforms were accompanied by the Union Conferences passing resolutions on political subjects, but these were blandly ignored by the party leaders. 'The action of the Conference', in Lowell's famous phrase, 'is not fettered; it is ignored' [143, i *p. 577*]. In the later nineteenth century the organisation of the Conservative Party was in fact run harmoniously by three men: Lord Salisbury, the Prime Minister, Akers-Douglas, the Chief Whip, and Captain Middleton. Middleton was both party agent and Secretary of the National Union between 1886 and 1903; and, by linking up the two principal sections of the party organisation – tactfully and skilfully – with the Parliamentary Party, the Conservative organisation reached, during these years, virtually technical perfection. The ascendancy of this remarkable triumvirate meant that the principle of 'authority' within the Conservative Party, never seriously in doubt, had finally triumphed.

So too with the Liberal Party. The fact that the National Liberal Federation remained loyal to Gladstone after 1886, and that thereafter Schnadhorst combined the posts of Secretary of the Federation and the Liberal Central Office until his retirement in 1894, did help to bring the central and local organisations of the Liberal Party closer together. On the other hand, the secession of the Whigs in 1886 led to a rising tide of Radicalism in the party which Gladstone was unable to stem, and this was reflected in the growing attempt by the National Liberal Federation to formulate and commit the party leaders to a definite programme. The high-water mark of this attitude was the famous 'Newcastle Programme' of 1891: a long and rambling series of resolutions which the Federation hoped would be passed into law by the next Liberal government, 'embodying Reforms which have been declared again and again by this Council to be essential to the welfare of the people of the United Kingdom' [143, i *p. 536*]. Gladstone did, after 1892, legislate on some of the proposals, though he never explicitly endorsed the programme. The programme, however, was felt to be an embarrassment to the Liberal government, and Rosebery, when he succeeded Gladstone in 1894, denounced the whole conception of attempting to fetter the hands of the parliamentary leaders; indeed, he blamed the 'Newcastle Programme' for the downfall of the government in the following year. Thereafter, in the remaining years of the nineteenth century, while altering the rules of the National Liberal Federation to create a pretence of greater power, the Liberal leaders – like their Conservative counterparts – really secured their own control over the Liberal Party. 'Both are shams', said Lowell, commenting on the fate of the Union and the Federation, 'but with this difference, that the Conservative organisation is a transparent, and the Liberal an opaque, sham' [143, i *p. 584*].

4 THE LIBERAL CRISIS

Turning his back on an ungrateful nation, Gladstone retired as leader of the Liberal Party in 1875, determined to spend his remaining years in theological study and reflection. He was succeeded by a duumvirate: Lord Hartington was elected leader in the Commons, and Lord Granville continued as leader in the House of Lords. But though the Radicals had acquiesced in the election of Hartington – Forster was unacceptable owing to his education policy – it was clearly a victory for the conservative and aristocratic section of the Liberal Party. How then could the Radicals capture the party? The answer given by Joseph Chamberlain was, as we have seen, to extend and strengthen the system of Liberal Associations that had blossomed after the defeat of 1874, and eventually in 1877 to join them together into the National Liberal Federation.

Curiously, Gladstone attended the famous inaugural meeting of the Federation held at Birmingham on 31 May 1877 – in the very citadel of radical nonconformity. His presence there was a response to Chamberlain's invitation, and Chamberlain's motives in urging him to attend were transparently clear. He intended to reshape the Liberal Party in his own image, and the presence of Gladstone at the Birmingham meeting would help him to do that. As he told Dilke quite frankly: ' . . . at this time I can't help thinking he is our best card . . . if he were to come back for a few years (he can't continue in public life for very much longer) he would probably do much for us and pave the way for more' [41, i *p. 240*]. Chamberlain's conviction that Gladstone's retirement was always just around the corner was to betray him time and time again in the course of the next ten years, and to affect profoundly his own fate and that of the Liberal Party. Granville warned Gladstone against going: 'I presume', he wrote, 'that Chamberlain's object is not to reorganise the whole liberal party, but to strengthen the young liberal and more advanced portion of it, and to secure you willing or unwilling as its leader' [70, i *p. 41*].

Gladstone was not unaware of Chamberlain's motives and ambitions. 'A man worth watching and studying', he shrewdly noted, '... of great tenacity of purpose; expecting to play an historical part, and probably destined to it' [70, i *p. 43*]. But he argued in reply that any opportunity must be seized for hammering the Conservative Government [70, i *p. 42*], and in any case he had his own special reasons for going. For, in the previous year, abandoning his theological studies, he had, under pressure, emerged as the greatest supporter of the Bulgarian Agitation. He soon found, sadly, that his own front bench and official Anglicanism were lukewarm in support, whereas many Radicals and the whole of nonconformity were solidly behind him. This impressed Gladstone profoundly; he never forgot what he called their 'noble support', and in an article published a few months later, he described the nonconformists – in the famous phrase – as 'the backbone of the Liberal Party' [1 *p. 99*]. His visit to Birmingham in 1877 is, in a sense, a public gesture of support and appreciation for English nonconformity which did much to heal the rift that had developed between them over his earlier education policy. It is also something more. It is, as Shannon has argued in his book on the Bulgarian Agitation, in its attempt to rebuild that moral *rapport* with the masses that had been broken in 1874, a stage on the road to Midlothian and the resumption of the Liberal leadership [73].

The fundamental conflict between Whigs and Radicals, already emerging during the Bulgarian Agitation of 1876, became more defined in the years preceding the general election of 1880. It was symbolised perhaps by Lord Hartington's distaste for the National Liberal Federation, and his refusal to address its annual meeting in 1878, despite Chamberlain's veiled threat: 'Can the leader of the liberal party afford to ignore altogether so large a section of it? If he does, the organisation will necessarily tend more and more to separate from official Liberalism and to form a party within the party, [47, i *pp. 246–7*]. One must not exaggerate, however, the differences between the two Liberal leaders in practice, as both realised the importance of party unity if the next general election was to be won. Lord Hartington did in fact go out of his way to conciliate the Radical pressure groups; and, in a speech to the National Liberal Federation at this time, Chamberlain asserted that 'The great need of the Liberal party at the present moment is union

. . . everything must give way to that' [60 *p. 125*]. Nevertheless, when the election did come in 1880, the Radicals believed they had two advantages *vis-à-vis* the Whigs. First, the control of the National Liberal Federation; secondly, the support of Gladstone who was now regarded as almost an 'honorary Radical'. The results of the election seemed to offer them the fulfilment of their hopes. The Liberals obtained a majority of 137 over the Conservatives, and the success in many boroughs could be attributed partly to the work of the National Liberal Federation. 'The old Whigs are astonished and bewildered', wrote Frederic Harrison to Charles Dilke. 'They have not won the victory. It has been forced on them by the Radicals, almost against their will. . . . Gladstone must give support to the Left whether he wishes it or not' (Frederic Harrison Papers (London School of Economics)).

In this he was over-sanguine. For the fundamental fact about the general election of 1880 from the point of view of the Liberal Party was that it was 'Mr Gladstone's victory'; and, as he himself said, 'it made me again leader whether I would or no' [66, ii *p. 158*]. Lord Hartington, the official party leader, reluctantly bowed to the inevitable, and, despite the hostility of the queen, it was Gladstone who now became Prime Minister for the second time. The enormous prestige he had built up since 1876 enabled him therefore to bypass the Radical programme and bend the Liberal Party to his own will. This was something which Lord Hartington would never have had the strength to do if he had continued as leader; and Gladstone's triumph in 1880 was, therefore, in Shannon's phrase, 'the ruin of Radicalism' [73 *p. 273*]. This was indeed implied almost as soon as Gladstone formed his new government. For, given his continuing predilection for the old aristocratic governing caste, only one member of his Cabinet of eleven was a full-blown Radical, Chamberlain at the Board of Trade, and Dilke had to make do with the Under-Secretaryship at the Foreign Office. Even these appointments were made reluctantly and with an ill grace. 'From this one-sided start', says Ensor, 'much of Gladstone's failure in his 1880–85 administration may be traced. For never in the modern era has a triumphant House of Commons majority achieved so little' [5 *pp. 66–7*].

It was this that disenchanted the Radicals with Gladstone within a few years of the great victory of 1880. It is true that there were special reasons for the Prime Minister's tardiness as a reformer. The situation now was very different from what it was in 1868. Gladstone's return to office in 1880 was, as he insisted, due to special circumstances; and if the electoral triumph of that year was his personal victory, it was a victory won against 'Beaconsfieldism' rather than for anything positive, concerned with foreign and imperial rather than domestic issues. The Liberal Party came into power in 1880 with no definite programme other than a vague commitment to franchise and local government reform. Indeed, Gladstone himself thought only in terms of clearing up one or two outstanding problems inherited from his predecessor – mainly in imperial affairs – before returning once again to the peace and quiet of Hawarden. His teasing obsession with old age and retirement – he was now seventy – added yet another element of uncertainty to the problems of the ministry. It helps to account for the 'plots' against Gladstone's leadership which some historians have discerned [35]; and contributed, in Matthew's phrase, to 'the curious stop–go quality of his second administration' [63, ii *p. 107*]. Moreover, Gladstone soon found that he was faced with problems both in Ireland and overseas which were not only of extraordinary complexity but charged with emotional dynamite; and in the Commons there were the wearying and time-consuming tactics of the Irish and the 'Fourth party', as well as the long-drawn-out problem of 'the Bradlaugh Case'. Prior to 1884 none of the great domestic policies of the Radicals – disestablishment, franchise reform, land purchase, tax changes, local government reform – had been accomplished; Chamberlain had even failed to carry his Merchant Shipping Bill through the Commons.

For many Radicals, even more disillusioning than the government's sins of omission were their sins of commission. It was the government's coercive policy in Ireland in 1881–82 that many found particularly repugnant: they were even more strongly opposed to what appeared to be a continuation of Disraeli's imperialism in South Africa and, more egregiously, in Egypt and the Sudan. In South Africa the government at first hesitated to restore independence to the Transvaal after the successful conclusion of the Zulu war in 1879. But the shock of of the Boer uprising and the British defeat at Majuba Hill in February 1881, together with pressure from the Radicals in the government, pushed Gladstone towards a quick settlement, and the Boers gained their independence subject to a vague British suzereignty, in the same year. Thus, in the Transvaal conciliation appeared to have triumphed. In Egypt, on the other hand, a quick, neat solution seemed beyond the government's grasp. There, British influence had already increased under the previous Conservative Administration. Ironically, it was the Liberals

who now blundered into direct military intervention in Egypt in
1882. This was the result of a confused and often contradictory set
of motives – strategic, financial and humanitarian – following the
outbreak of a nationalist revolt in the country, the withdrawal of
the French, and the deaths of about fifty Europeans in anti-foreign
riots in Alexandria. As a result of General Wolseley's victory at
Tel-el-Kebir the Liberal government found itself, to its own
astonishment and embarrassment, the master of Egypt. The
occupation of Egypt produced a real moral crisis for the Liberal
Party: how could armed intervention against a native people be
justified on Liberal principles? Indeed on this issue there was no
clearcut Whig – Radical division; the Radicals themselves were bitterly
divided – a portent of what was to come in the 1890s. Chamberlain,
though he disliked the reasons for it, supported Hartington in
favour of intervention, just as earlier he had in the end supported
coercion in Ireland; while Radical anti-imperialists like John Morley
were strongly against any such action, and John Bright, consistent to
the last, resigned from the government after the bombardment of
Alexandria in 1882. These were views with which Gladstone himself
– a reluctant imperialist – was sympathetic. Hartington believed
that, over the Egyptian question, the government was 'in imminent
danger of being broken up', and he urged upon Gladstone the duty
of carrying on as Premier: 'your retirement would lead to the
speedy, if not the immediate, dissolution of the Government and of
the present Liberal majority' [47, i *pp. 364, 378*].

   Gladstone had no intention of retiring. The government was
reconstructed, and Dilke was brought into the Cabinet as President
of the Local Government Board. This did little to pacify the
Radicals. 'The Radicals in the Cabinet', Chamberlain wrote of the
year 1883, 'were now only Dilke and myself and we found our
views ignored or outvoted by the majority of our colleagues. In the
country, however, our opinions were endorsed by at least four-fifths
of the Liberal Party' [32 *p. 86*]. It was this that led many Radicals
in the country to demand a more vigorous campaign by
Chamberlain against the domination of the Whigs. But Chamberlain
believed that there were sound reasons for his refusal to force things
to an issue with the Hartingtons and Granvilles. The Radicals were
still a minority in the Cabinet and in the Parliamentary Party; and –
like the Whigs also – they still needed, as Edward Hamilton
observed, 'Mr G's aegis to be spread over them' [50 *p. 167*].
Chamberlain's plan, therefore, was to postpone the battle for
control of the party until a general election could be fought, after

the passing of a new Reform Act; then, with the country labourers enfranchised and the constituencies remodelled, the Radicals could dominate the party and he would emerge as party leader, for Gladstone was then bound to retire. Chamberlain's plan worked, almost. For when the Reform Acts *were* passed in 1884–85, the establishment of single-member constituencies – which ended the old practice by which a Whig and a Radical were often run together in two-member constituencies – did mark, *vis-à-vis* the Whigs, a Radical triumph, though it probably helped the Conservatives even more. What the editor of the Radical *Fortnightly* called the 'Revolution of 1884' meant, as he affirmed, that 'the buffers on which timid Liberalism has hitherto relied against advanced Liberalism will henceforth disappear' [38].

If the Radicals were soon disenchanted with Gladstone, so too, for very different reasons, were many Whigs. Suspicious already, even before the formation of his Second Ministry, of Gladstone's pandering to the masses, especially during the Midlothian Campaign of 1879–80, they were also alarmed at the effects of the Second Irish Land Act of 1881 which, like Lord Hartington, the great landowners found 'a hard morsel to swallow' [47, i *p. 340*]. Not only did it attack the landlords' just rights in Ireland, but its likely effects in England were even more alarming. For there the landlords were already under fire politically from every species of land reformer – in the spirit of Chamberlain's famous denunciation of them in 1883 as 'the class that toil not neither do they spin' – at the very moment when, economically, they were hit by fierce agricultural depression [163]. Nor indeed was it only the landed interest that found itself menaced by the spirit of Gladstone's legislation. A representative of the important 'city interest' in the Liberal Party like Goschen (who had ostentatiously refused to join the government in 1880) was equally uneasy, as indeed were many small property owners, an important factor in the Conservative reaction of the later nineteenth century.

The year 1885 saw, therefore, what was in many respects an intense struggle between the Whigs and Radicals for control of the Liberal Party, a struggle which was worsened by Gladstone's increasing lack of control over his Cabinet and the Parliamentary Liberal Party [70 *intro*]. This was accompanied in the early part of the year, by tentative moves within the Cabinet aimed at replacing the Prime Minister and establishing a Hartington Administration which both Chamberlain and Dilke were prepared to support [35]. This was a response to the apparent collapse of Gladstone's political

morale, and his health, as a result of the agonising problems of
Egyptian finance, and General Gordon and the Sudan. The Prime
Minister had no appreciation of the tremendous hold the general
had established over the British public as a result of the news of his
lonely stand against the Mahdi's rebel forces at Khartoum until his
final capture and murder in January 1885. Gordon's death was
blamed – not entirely fairly – on Gladstone's tardiness in sending a
relief expedition. These events delivered another shattering blow to
the reputation of the government, already battered by divisions over
Ireland and parliamentary reform. In a censure motion in the
Commons at the end of February the government's majority fell to
just fourteen, and Gladstone contemplated resigning. By the spring,
however, following the capture of Khartoum by the rebels and the
British decision to abandon the Sudan, Gladstone had recovered his
nerve, and thrusting aside all thoughts of retirement he now
reasserted his authority over the Cabinet. Indeed, he now came to
believe that his retention of the leadership would alone serve to
maintain unity within the Liberal Party. In May, however,
Chamberlain and Dilke tendered their resignations over the question
of renewing the Irish Crimes Bill; but this action was overtaken by
events when, a few weeks later, the government was defeated by a
combination of Irish and Conservative votes, with more than
seventy Liberals abstaining. Gladstone resigned, and was succeeded
by a Conservative 'caretaker government' under Lord Salisbury
until, when the new electoral lists had been compiled, a general
election could be held.

The election campaign at the end of the year was virtually a
personal duel between Lord Hartington and Joseph Chamberlain, a
duel in which the Radical set the pace. For Chamberlain, aware of
the disappointments of his supporters with the achievements of the
government of which he had been a prominent member, now hoped
to renew their morale with a campaign for a definite 'Radical
Programme' [31] This programme was developed in detail in a great
cycle of speeches throughout the country in 1885. Chamberlain
supported such policies as disestablishment of the Church of
England, land reform, free education, local government reform and
progressive taxation; and, in highly provocative language, he made
taunting references to the 'rights of property'. All this was
disconcerting to Gladstone who was uneasy about Chamberlain's
methods and loath to see the party committed to such definite
policies [*Doc. 21*]. Chamberlain's original Radical programme,
however, was considerably modified in the course of the year until,

during the election, under the sobriquet of the 'Unauthorised Programme', it consisted for Chamberlain of three major points: local government reform, land reform, and free education [48]. On paper, this did not differ all that much from Gladstone's 'Authorised' programme published in September, which also included proposals on local government and land reform, but it was interpreted as a sop to the Whigs. 'It is a slap in the face to us', wrote Chamberlain to Dilke. 'His reign cannot be a long one. . . . If we chose to go into direct opposition we might smash him but the game is not worth the candle' [41, ii *p. 96*].

The Whigs, however, were still alarmed, professing to see in Chamberlain's proposals the spectre of 'Socialism', though Chamberlain – who believed profoundly that his proposed reforms would stimulate individual, and especially local, effort – was not really a Socialist at all [40 *p. 46*]. In reply to Chamberlain's attacks Lord Hartington defended the 'rights of property' in a notable speech at Waterfoot in August; and in October he wrote despondently, but prophetically, to Granville: 'Of course in the long run the active men will have their own way and the future Liberal Party will be Radical. I see nothing for the Whigs but to disappear or turn Tories' [47, ii *p. 74*]. That sea-change was not to take place, yet. For though Gladstone was in many ways antipathetic to Chamberlain – 'his socialism repels me,' he said – he was perhaps even more disillusioned with the conduct of 'the timid or reactionary Whigs' [66, ii *pp. 461–2*]. He tried desperately, therefore, with his mind already turning towards Ireland, to maintain at least some semblance of unity in the party; and the final showdown between Chamberlain and the Whigs failed to take place before the Liberals faced the general election of November 1885. 'The problem for me', wrote Gladstone, 'is to make if possible a statement which will hold through the election, and not to go into conflict with either the right wing of the party, for whom Hartington has spoken, or the left wing . . . for whom Chamberlain spoke' [39 *p. 229*].

That election – one of the oddest in modern British political history – did little to rejoice the hearts of either Whigs, Radicals or Conservatives. The final figures were: Liberal 335, Conservatives 249, Irish 86; and the real victor was Parnell, who had not only obtained his primary aim – to hold the balance of power in the House of Commons – but had utterly destroyed the power of the Liberal Party in Ireland into the bargain. One of the outstanding features of the election from the Liberals' point of view was their heavy losses in the boroughs. It is true that they still maintained their lead in the largest industrial cities, but in London, Lancashire and the smaller boroughs generally they did badly. This was due to a variety of causes. Lord Grosvenor, the Chief Whip, believed that Chamberlain's 'extremism' had 'frightened away shoals' of floating voters [51 *p. 116*]; certainly recent historians find his electoral campaign in 1885 curiously inept [24; 35; 151].

Gladstone himself wrote to Grosvenor that the main factors were: 'Fair Trade + Parnell + Church + Chamberlain . . . I place the *causae damni* in what I think their order of importance' [45 *p. 398*]. This was a fair estimate. The Catholic workingmen in England obediently voted Conservative in accordance with Parnell's instructions, and this was particularly important in Lancashire. 'Free schools' was especially unpopular owing to its link with increased taxation. But there is also some evidence to suggest that the industrial working classes in the cities were strongly influenced by the unsatisfactory state of trade; and it is worth emphasising that many of them saw Joseph Chamberlain not so much as the supporter of the 'Unauthorised Programme' (in which they had little interest) but as the ex-President of the Board of Trade who had done little to improve their prospects of employment. Nor was it only the fact that he had no 'urban cow' (in Labouchère's famous phrase) to offer them that accounts for the coolness of the workers towards Chamberlain: most of their leaders had resented him from the start. 'The Radical today', said J. E. Williams of the Social Democratic Federation, 'was the "Artful Dodger" who went up and down the country telling the people to take hold of the landlord thief but to let the greater thief, the capitalist, go scotfree' [165 *p. 53*].

In the counties, on the other hand, the Liberals did remarkably well: in England and Wales their numbers went up from 54 in 1880 to 133 in 1885 – giving them about thirty more county seats than their Conservative opponents. This is generally attributed to Chamberlain's wooing of the agricultural labourer – enfranchised in 1884 – with his land policy, the famous 'three acres and a cow'; but Henry Pelling is more sceptical. He believes that the growing Conservative support of protection was more important, and the agricultural labourer voted Liberal 'more out of fear of fiscal change, which might increase the cost of living, than because of any positive attraction of Chamberlain's social programme' [149 *p. 16*]. Clearly, bread and butter issues were again of major importance in an election. It was Irish policy, however, that determined what party should now govern. Immediately after the election in November Lord Salisbury, with the tacit support of the Irish Party, carried on as Prime Minister. But in December Herbert Gladstone flew his 'Hawarden Kite' and announced to a startled world the news of his father's conversion to Home Rule. Soon after Parliament reassembled in January 1886, therefore, the Irish switched their votes and Gladstone, at the age of seventy-seven, became Prime Minister for the third time, committed in fact, if not yet formally, to a policy of Home Rule for Ireland.

IRELAND

It had taken Gladstone many years of anguish and reflection before he reached the conclusion that Home Rule was the only solution for the Irish problem. Though he took up the Irish question in 1868 as a response to the Fenian outrages and as a device for uniting his party, he did so also, as he told his sister, 'in the name of the God of truth and justice' [59 p. 192]. It is his concern with 'justice for Ireland' that is the *leitmotiv* of J. L. Hammond's classic study of 'Gladstone and the Irish Nation' [45]. The aim of Gladstone's early Irish reforms was simply 'to pacify Ireland': to wipe out specific grievances by legislative action and thus justify to the Irish people the wisdom of the Union. Gladstone believed that his Church Act (1869) and his Land Act (1870) had helped to achieve this, and he remained supremely optimistic about the future of the Union. This was so even though the foundation of the Irish Home Rule Party in 1873 showed that piecemeal reform alone was no longer acceptable to Irish nationalists. Gladstone's approach to the Irish question in the later 1870s remained the same, despite the outbreak of the Land War between tenants and landlords and the foundation of the Irish Land League in 1879. In that year his thoughts were centred on conflicts that were taking place much farther afield than on the other side of the Irish Sea.

Hence when Gladstone assumed the premiership for the second time in 1880, he was still thinking in terms of clearing up one or two difficult problems, mainly in foreign and imperial affairs, before returning to that 'quiet and unobtrusive life' (as he expressed it to Rosebery in 1878) from which he had been so rudely snatched in 1876. As he admitted frankly in 1884 with reference to Ireland: 'I did not know, no one knew, the severity of the crisis that was already swelling upon the horizon, and that shortly after rushed upon us like a flood' [66, ii p. 288]. What changed his attitude after 1880 was his growing awareness that in Ireland the government faced not just a 'political' but a 'social' revolution as a result of the activities of the Land League [66, ii *p. 287*]. The only long-term solution to this, as he insisted in opposition to Forster, the Irish Secretary, was not the imprisonment of a handful of so-called agitators, but large-scale land and local government reform. 'Until we have', he told the Irish Secretary in 1882, 'seriously responsible bodies to deal with us in Ireland, every plan we frame comes to Irishmen . . . as an English plan. As such it is probably condemned. . . . It is liberty alone which fits men for liberty' [66, ii *p. 298*]. It is from sentiments such as these that we can already discern the shadowy outlines of Gladstone's later Home Rule policy.

Nevertheless, Gladstone came to accept that as the situation in Ireland was now so desperate special powers were needed to deal with it, and early in 1881 a tough new Coercion Bill was introduced into the House of Commons. Though this was 'obstructed' by the Irish Parliamentary Party and its new leader, Charles Stewart Parnell, for forty-one hours continuously, it was eventually passed. This Act gave the authorities in Ireland special powers of arrest and imprisonment; and as a result Michael Davitt, the leader of the Land League, was arrested and imprisoned without trial. Coercion, however, was accompanied by reform: a few months later Gladstone passed his Second Land Act. This granted the major demands of the Irish tenants – the '3 Fs': (1) 'Fair Rents', which were to be fixed for fifteen years by special Land Courts; (2) 'Fixity of Tenure', which meant that tenants could not be evicted if they paid their rents; (3) 'Free Sale', which recognised the tenant's 'interest' in his holding and his right to compensation when he relinquished it. Gladstone's main purpose in his Second Land Act was to destroy the *raison d'être* of the Land League and thus end the violence in Ireland, by granting the League's main demands. For the moment, however, Parnell refused to co-operate in the carrying out of the Act. Forster therefore had him arrested and imprisoned in Kilmainham Gaol in Dublin.

Paradoxically, Parnell's arrest was the prelude to better relations between the Irish leader and the British government. Gladstone realised that the arrest of Parnell solved nothing: violence inevitably increased during his six months incarceration. Parnell, on his side, perceived that the situation in Ireland had changed dramatically. The Land Act was winning out over the Land League. Irish tenants – defying the views of their extremists – were now using the new Land Courts to get their rents reduced legally, and the Land War was effectively grinding to a halt. For Parnell, therefore, there was much to be said for coming to terms with the Liberals and returning to his essential role as the leader of a constitutional Irish Party, committed to obtaining Home Rule through the parliamentary process. All the conditions were thus present for an agreement between Gladstone and Parnell. With Chamberlain acting as an intermediary, what became known as the 'Kilmainham Treaty' was quickly concluded in April 1882. By its terms the government agreed to release Parnell and relax the Coercion Act, and to bring within the terms of the Land Act those tenants in arrears with their rents. Parnell for his part agreed to use his influence against violence, accept and support the work of the Land Courts, and co-operate in the future with the Liberal Party. All this was too much for Forster, who resigned in disgust. The new accord between Parnell and the Liberals was shaken but not irretrievably damaged by the brutal murder of Lord Frederick Cavendish (Forster's successor as Irish Secretary) and T. H. Burke, the Under-Secretary, in Phoenix Park, Dublin, on 6 May, by an Irish revolutionary group. A new Coercion Act (to last for three years) was hurriedly passed.

The sincere shock and horror displayed by Parnell over the Phoenix Park murders created a favourable impression in the House of Commons, and he remained on good terms with Gladstone. Now Parnell really was the master of the Irish Parliamentary Party and the 'uncrowned King of Ireland'. He was soon courted by both Liberals and Conservatives since both groups recognised that his Irish Party might well hold the balance of power in the House of Commons after the next general election. This was due to take place some time in 1885, after the new electoral lists had been compiled following the passage of the Third Reform Act of 1884. Joseph Chamberlain was first off the mark. At the end of 1884, in order to obtain Parnell's support, he proposed to him a 'Central Board' scheme for Ireland which would have given the Irish wide-ranging powers of internal control. For the English Radical this was conceived as an alternative to Home Rule; but on those terms it had no possible chance of being accepted by Parnell. In January 1885, in one of his most powerful speeches in Ireland, Parnell reiterated his commitment to Home Rule. Chamberlain's scheme was in any case rejected by the Cabinet, despite Gladstone's support.

Gladstone's Irish policy, therefore, during his Second Ministry, though well-meaning, failed on two counts. It failed on the one hand, despite the merits of individual measures like the Second Land Act or the proposed extension of local government, to satisfy the national aspirations of the Irish people; while, on the other hand, every major Irish proposal introduced served only to exacerbate animosities and disagreements within the Liberal Cabinet. By the time the ministry came to an end in June 1885, therefore, Gladstone was convinced that traditional Liberal policy towards Ireland was completely bankrupt.

It was this that helped to make the summer months of 1885 the key period in Gladstone's conversion to Home Rule. His own policy of religious and agrarian reform had failed to reconcile the Irish to the continuance of English rule; further reform was bound to be just as nugatory. Moreover, Gladstone's reflection during these months on the fundamentals of the Irish attitude, coupled with his deep 'European' outlook, convinced him of the reality of Irish nationality: how then could he oppose what a majority of the Irish people wanted [*Doc. 22*]? His letters to Hartington and Chamberlain in September, and his conversations with Lord Derby later, showed that it was perfectly plain to them that his mind was moving to a definite Home Rule policy [45 *pp. 404–6*]. The problem for Gladstone was – what tactics should he now pursue? In the end he determined, publicly, to maintain silence over his conversion to Home Rule. Why? Gladstone seems to have been moved primarily by two considerations. In the first place, if he spoke out publicly in favour of Home Rule the break-up of the Liberal Party would inevitably follow, and on the eve of a general election; in addition, he could be accused of counterbidding for the Irish vote. Secondly, as J. L. Hammond has argued, Gladstone aimed, sincerely if naïvely, at achieving a non-party approach to the Irish problem. The Conservatives had after all come into power in June 1885 as a result of Parnell's conviction that he could get more from them than from the Liberals. As a result, coercion was dropped, a land purchase policy *was* successfully inaugurated; might not this lead on therefore – following feelers put out by Carnarvon, the Irish Viceroy – to a Conservative policy of Home Rule? Gladstone realised, moreover, the enormous advantages for the success of a Home Rule policy if it was introduced by Lord Salisbury, with his mastery of the House of Lords, backed up by the majority of Liberals. 'Every step he took between June 1885 and January 1886', writes J. L. Hammond, 'was a deliberate effort to obtain a solution by passionless cooperation among the leading statesmen' [45 *p. 471*]. It was these considerations that led Gladstone to keep silent, even to Parnell and his colleagues, during the election campaign at the end of the year, and to acquiesce in Irish support for the Conservative Party.

The outcome of the election of 1885 was a disappointment for Gladstone in so far as it failed to provide either of the English parties with a real majority independent of the Irish members. On the other hand, the fact that the Irish Party won every seat in Ireland south of Ulster clinched his support for Home Rule. 'I consider that Ireland has now spoken', he wrote to Hartington on 17 December, 'and that an effort ought to be made *by the government* without delay to meet her demands for the management by an Irish legislative body of Irish as distinct from imperial affairs. Only a government can do it, and a tory government can do it more easily and safely than any other' [*66, ii p. 503*]. Gladstone's hope, however, was utterly destroyed by the publication on the very same day of the news of his support for Home Rule, as a result of the deliberate action of his son, Herbert Gladstone. Herbert believed that Chamberlain and his Radical friends were planning to take over the Liberal Party, and the only way to forestall them was by flying the 'Hawarden Kite' and forcing his father to re-enter the political arena. In this he was successful. As a result, it was Gladstone and not Salisbury who faced the formidable task of forming a government at the end of January to introduce Home Rule for Ireland, a task he accepted with alacrity. These events have led John Vincent and A. B. Cooke, in their major study of British parliamentary politics in 1885–86, to argue that, for Gladstone, 'Ireland was viewed in a context of deep party calculation' [*35 p. 55*]. They suggest that Gladstone's support for Home Rule at this time was due to opportunism rather than conviction; it was primarily an attempt to re-unite the Liberal Party under his own leadership and thus put paid to the ambitions of Joseph Chamberlain. 'The [Home Rule Bill]', they write, 'was meant to unite the Liberal Party by committing it to the principle of home rule and to prepare it for further protracted struggle in which there would be only one possible leader' [*35 p. 55*]. The whole argument is highly controversial, and now seems difficult to sustain. For though we can accept that Gladstone was inevitably concerned with the future of the Liberal Party in 1885–86, there is abundant evidence that he was committed to Home Rule before the general election of November 1885; and, more recently, a number of historians have argued powerfully that it is impossible to understand Gladstone's politics without constant reference to his moral and religious outlook [*4; 75*].

The task that now confronted Gladstone was one undertaken in the worst possible circumstances since nearly all his colleagues had been left completely in the dark about his change of attitude. Hartington and most of the ex-Whig ministers refused to join him;

Chamberlain and Trevelyan did so reluctantly, but resigned in March once the Home Rule Bill was introduced before the Cabinet. That Bill aimed to establish an elected Parliament for the whole of Ireland with considerable powers of internal self-government, and the Irish representation at Westminster was to end. 'What happened in 1886', writes J. L. Hammond, 'was exactly the opposite of what Gladstone wanted in 1885. . . . For the crisis created a combination, but a combination not to obtain reform but to defeat it' [45 *pp. 456–7*]. This it did in June 1886 when ninety-three Liberal Unionists, led by Lord Hartington and Joseph Chamberlain, combined with the Conservatives in the House of Commons to defeat the Home Rule Bill, which was lost by thirty votes. How are we to explain their opposition?

The orthodox view is that the Liberal Unionist opposition to Home Rule represented the culmination of that 'Revolt of the Whigs' against Gladstonian Liberalism which, so it has been argued, had been proceeding since at least the beginning of Gladstone's Second Ministry [122]. Sixty Whig peers revolted against the government over the Irish Compensation Bill in 1880, entitling us, says Professor Southgate, 'to regard the vote as a rehearsal by the Whig peerage of its exit from the Liberal ranks, which so many saw as a matter of time only' [76 *p. 372*]. Lord Lansdowne resigned from the government in 1880; the Duke of Argyle a year later over the Land Bill, and Lord Cowper (and W. E. Forster) in 1882. Home Rule was thus the occasion rather than the cause of the split in the Liberal Party, for it seemed the apotheosis of all those features of contemporary 'democracy' – and especially the increasing domination of the popular will over intellect and experience – about which the Whigs and many moderate Liberals were most uneasy. Moreover the Whigs felt that they were fighting a losing battle with the Radicals within the party. 'What Home Rule did', writes Southgate, 'was to turn the growing tide of seceders into a flood by presenting a major and dramatic issue' [76 *p. 414*]. The Whig secession in 1886 was thus, according to this view, more or less inevitable.

Some recent historians are critical of this whole thesis. They point to the obvious fact that the Whigs were not the only opponents of Home Rule in 1886. Though they formed the largest group among the dissidents (more than forty MPs out of ninety-three), about thirty Liberal Unionists were businessmen, and some twenty were lawyers. Gladstone therefore also lost much support in 1886 from the moderates within the Parliamentary Party. Moreover, the notion of a general 'Whig Revolt' against Gladstone before 1886 is something of a myth; only a handful of ministerial resignations did occur and these were confined almost entirely to members of the House of Lords. Nor does there appear to be any correlation between the behaviour of the Liberal Unionists in 1886 and their attitude towards government policy before that date. Even the most controversial of measures during the Second Ministry – notably, the 1881 Irish Land Bill and the Reform Bills of 1884 and 1885 – were in the end supported by the overwhelming majority of the ninety-three dissidents, including the Whigs, who later voted against the government over Home Rule. The voting record of the Liberal Unionists before 1885 was practically indistinguishable from that of their Gladstonian colleagues [56]. The Whigs in fact played their customary role in the counties on behalf of the Liberal Party in the general election of November 1885; and indeed, owing to the failures of Chamberlainite Radicalism in that contest, it has been suggested that the Whigs probably emerged from the election in a stronger position than they had been earlier [54]. Lord Hartington himself – though he was wearied and disillusioned with the confusions and conflicts of the previous ministry – was confident that the Whigs still had an important part to play within the Liberal Party [53]. He regarded himself – and was so regarded – as Gladstone's inevitable successor.

The conclusion drawn from all this evidence by recent historians is that Liberal Unionist opposition to Home Rule was not based on socio-economic factors but on 'genuine ideological reasons' [54 *p. 214*]. In particular, the Liberal Unionists argued that Home Rule would inevitably lead to complete separation by Ireland and therefore the break-up of the United Kingdom, especially as the Irish would no longer be represented at Westminster. This would have disastrous consequences, both for the prosperity of the British and Irish people, and for the future of the British Empire as a whole. The Liberal Unionists also resented Gladstone's refusal to open his mind to them frankly over his conversion to Home Rule, and the authoritarian and emotional leadership style he adopted during the period that led up to the introduction of his Home Rule Bill in April 1886. It was, therefore, suggests Parry, 'the determination of Gladstone to stay in charge and to re-define Liberalism around Home Rule' that was the primary cause of the disruption of 1886 [69 *p. 302*].

One can understand why Lord Hartington was moved by all these considerations to oppose Home Rule. The real problem is Joseph

Chamberlain, and his behaviour in the Home Rule crisis is the most puzzling and controversial of all. For Joseph Chamberlain was after all a Radical, in Irish as well as in domestic affairs. It was Chamberlain who in 1881 originally supported Gladstone in opposing Forster's proposed Coercion Bill, and in the following year acted as a link between the Cabinet and Parnell in arranging the 'Kilmainham Treaty'. It was Chamberlain further who, in 1885, was the principal opponent within the Cabinet of an unconditional renewal of the Irish Crimes Act, and who attempted, through the Irish MP, Captain O'Shea, to obtain Parnell's agreement to a Central Board Scheme which would give the Irish wide-ranging powers of internal control [76 *pp. 366–7*]. It was indeed over Irish affairs that he and Dilke tendered their resignations in May of that year.

Why then was it Chamberlain of all people who allied with his old Whig enemy, Hartington, in 1886, to oppose Gladstone's Home Rule Bill? A number of points may be suggested. In the first place, it is impossible to ignore the factor of personality. Though each recognised the high qualities of the other, there was that lack of real sympathy and understanding between Gladstone and Chamberlain which was bound to make agreement more difficult in dealing with the intractable problems of Ireland; and the fault here lies mainly with Gladstone. The 'Grand Old Man' was tactless and insensitive in his relations with his younger colleague. He was loath to admit him to the Cabinet in 1880; in 1882 he twice failed to consider him for the post of Irish Secretary when in many ways Chamberlain would have been an admirable choice; even in 1885, when Chamberlain was anxious to become Colonial Secretary, he was first absurdly offered the Admiralty, and then given the Local Government Board but without any strong backing for a policy of social reform. All this meant not only that Chamberlain felt, with considerable justification, that he was being slighted at the behest of the Whigs, but also that he was not bound by the same ties of personal devotion and loyalty to Gladstone which characterised the behaviour of many Liberals in 1886, including even a Whig like Granville.

But quite apart from personal differences, the two men looked at Ireland in fundamentally different ways. Gladstone did eventually attempt, if with only partial success, to see Irish problems through Irish eyes; Chamberlain made no real attempt to view Ireland other than as an Englishman, and a nonconformist at that. What Chamberlain increasingly emphasised after 1881 was not the causes but the harsh reality of Irish crime and violence, and the callousness and duplicity of the Irish leaders [*Doc. 23*]. Implicit in Chamberlain's approach, therefore, was the view that the Irish were unfit to govern themselves – at least in important matters; and this view appeared to be confirmed by Parnell's double-dealing over the Central Board Scheme (though the fault here lay with O'Shea), and his untrustworthiness in switching the Irish vote in the 1885 election. It is this almost instinctive belief in strong, efficient government at almost any price – as typical of his early Radical as of his later Conservative career – that helps to explain Chamberlain's attitude towards Home Rule. He was prepared to go far, as his Central Board Scheme shows, in giving the Irish what he believed they wanted: as he said, 'the widest possible self-government . . . consistent with the integrity of the Empire' [32 *p. 151*]; but, unlike Gladstone, he was not prepared to make the jump (and the gap seemed a very small one to many contemporaries) from devolution to Home Rule, even if a majority of Irishmen clearly wanted it. The disruption of the Empire which would, he argued, inevitably follow, was too high a price to pay. In any case he believed that such purely political considerations were really irrelevant. It was the land question that was 'the foundation of Irish . . . discontent and should be settled first' [32 *p. 229*].

There is one last point. How sincere, even in these terms, was Chamberlain's opposition to Home Rule? Chamberlain in his own *Political Memoir*, written mainly in 1892, sees himself as a man who put country and Empire before party loyalty and personal ambition in the crisis of 1886; and this is a view which his principal biographer, J. L. Garvin, follows. But it is difficult to believe that Joseph Chamberlain was not also conscious of the long-term political advantages of what he was doing – as more recent historians have implied; and once again his belief in the imminent retirement of Gladstone was crucial. For Chamberlain was well aware of the antipathy of the British public – and particularly the working-men – to the Irish, and therefore to Home Rule, a theme he constantly stressed in private correspondence throughout the 1880s. If the Liberal Party came out in support of Home Rule at a new general election, he suggested to Gladstone in 1885, 'it is my belief that we should sustain a tremendous defeat. The English working classes, for various reasons, are distinctly hostile to Home Rule carried to this extent' [32 *p. 171*]. Hence there was much to be said for the view that, if the Liberal train was bent on destruction, then it would be wise for Chamberlain, temporarily, to get off and come back later to take over the controls from Gladstone after his inevitable retirement. This interpretation certainly seems to be implicit in the important letter he wrote to his brother on 8 March 1886 [*Doc. 24*]. This view would imply further that he was determined to kill the Home Rule Bill come what may, and that Chamberlain's negotiations with Gladstone over its detailed provisions were a mere smokescreen. Indeed, he wrote to Dilke on 6 May 1886: 'To satisfy others I have talked about conciliation, and have consented to make advances, but on the whole I would rather vote against the Bill than not, and the retention of the Irish members is only with me, the flag that covers other objections' [45 *p. 495*]. In the end, of course, things did not work out quite as Chamberlain expected. The Home Rule Bill *was* defeated; the Unionists *did* win a great victory at the polls in the general election of July 1886; but the Grand Old Man stubbornly refused to bow to the inevitable. What destroyed Chamberlain's plans, therefore, was Gladstone's determination to carry on as Liberal leader after 1886, and the willpower and obstinacy that enabled him to do so for another eight years. By that time any hope of Chamberlain rejoining the Liberal Party had long since passed.

AFTER 1886

The decline of the Liberal Party is the major feature of Victorian political history between 1886 and the death of the queen. The facts seem to speak for themselves, though they are difficult to interpret. In the general election that followed the defeat of the Home Rule Bill in 1886 the Unionists won a resounding victory, winning 394 seats (316 Conservatives, 78 Liberal Unionists); the Gladstonian Liberals were reduced to 191, backed up by the Irish Party of 85 members. This verdict may reasonably be regarded as exceptional since it followed immediately upon the split in the Liberal Party. But even at the general election of 1892, though the Liberals increased their numbers, their parliamentary majority was obtained only by complete dependence on the Irish members: Liberals 273, Irish 81, Conservatives 269, Liberal Unionists 46. In the election of 1895, by which time the repercussions of Home Rule were practically dead, the Liberals suffered their worst defeat of the century. They lost about 100 seats, while the Conservatives and their Liberal Unionist allies obtained 411 seats, with an overall majority of 152. The 'Khaki Election' of 1900 barely altered the relative position of the parties. Two general features of the Liberal electoral position during this period are worth emphasising. First, their only parliamentary majority during this period, in 1892, was secured only with the direct support of the Irish Party and the indirect support of Welsh and Scottish voters; they failed to secure a majority of seats in English constituencies. Thereafter, their dependence on the 'Celtic fringe' became even greater, and they were unable to win a majority of English seats until 1906. Secondly, the weak parliamentary position of the Liberal Party after 1885 was not the consequence of a great slump in the Liberal vote; indeed, even in 1895 they polled nearly two million votes – a little less than in 1892 – and the Conservatives gained only 51 per cent of the total votes cast [126 p. 255]. The real trouble for the Liberals was that, unlike the Conservatives, they failed to enlarge their absolute poll at a time when the working-class electorate was rapidly increasing; and indeed the fact that the Liberal vote in 1906 was bumped up by about a million, suggests that many working-class 'Liberals' in the later nineteenth century just failed to turn out at elections [132] [Doc. 25].

How are we to explain these facts? One obvious explanation for the decline of the Liberal Party lies in the Home Rule crisis of 1886 and the secession of the Liberal Unionists which followed. Certainly the leadership of the party was dramatically affected, since at one blow both Hartington and Chamberlain were removed, and the prospective succession to Gladstone was drastically altered and, as soon became apparent, weakened. The G.O.M. himself carried on as the leader of the party, still determined to place Irish Home Rule first even if it meant dragging a reluctant rank-and-file along behind him and accepting as a *quid pro quo* the ragbag policies of the 'Newcastle Programme' [24]. 'The defects of his strength grow on him', wrote Rosebery. 'All black is very black, all white very white' [50 p. 196]. But for the English people Gladstone was still, despite his growing remoteness from political realities, the personification of English Liberalism; and after the election of 1892 he became Prime Minister for the fourth time, determined to introduce yet another Home Rule Bill. The Second Bill passed through the Commons in 1893, but was crushed overwhelmingly in the Lords. Gladstone would have liked to dissolve and appeal to the country, as in 1886, but his colleagues – divided by their own personal animosities and strained almost beyond endurance by the G.O.M.'s contemptuous treatment of them – refused to agree; and Gladstone carried on as Premier for another seven wretched months, growing ever more oracular, aloof, embittered, and impossible to work with. The end came in March 1894 when Gladstone, at odds with the whole Cabinet over the naval estimates, at last reluctantly retired [*Doc. 26*].

The Liberal Cabinet now faced the extraordinarily difficult problem of finding a successor 'Talk of the Liberal party?' said John Morley, 'why, it consists of Mr. G. After him it will disappear and all will be chaos' [4 *p. 41*]. In effect the choice was between the Chancellor of the Exchequer, Sir William Harcourt, a man of considerable parliamentary experience and ability, but of an abrasive personality, and the Foreign Secretary, Lord Rosebery, with John Morley, the Irish Secretary, as third runner and go-between. In the end Rosebery emerged as victor, mainly because, despite the obvious weaknesses of his character and position, Harcourt was personally unendurable as Premier to all the Liberal front bench, and Rosebery was the queen's first choice. Thus, with his ex-rival and bitter enemy leading the party in the House of Commons, he entered upon his *damnosa hereditas*. 'The Liberal schism', Rosebery's latest biographer writes, 'opened the way to his succession as leader of the party by eliminating virtually all his rivals, but ensured that that leadership would be a precarious and compromised position' [50 *p. 191*]. That position, difficult from the start, soon became virtually intolerable, as Rosebery described to the queen in a bitter and revealing letter [*Doc. 27*]. It was his growing feeling of personal frustration and impotence, rather than the more fundamental weaknesses in the government and party, that led Rosebery to resign on a trivial issue in June 1895. The smash-up of the Liberal Party in the election that followed seemed a just verdict on a government that had revealed so nakedly its lack of unity, leadership or clearcut policies. 'The firm of Rosebery and Harcourt', as the former wrote to Gladstone with characteristic candour, 'was a fraud upon the public '[77 *p. 191*].

But no real attempt was made by the two men to overcome their differences in the course of the next year. The feud was in fact worsened by growing disputes over foreign and imperial policy in which Gladstone, launching a mini-crusade over Armenia, supported the anti-Rosebery faction: abruptly in October 1896 Rosebery resigned as leader of the Liberal Party. Harcourt, therefore, at last became *de facto* leader; but it soon became only too clear that he was incapable of remedying the deep-seated malaise that afflicted the Liberal Party [*Doc. 28*]. His inept performance over the Jameson Raid inquiry convinced his colleagues that he possessed none of the qualities of real leadership, and there were murmurings against him in the National Liberal Federation [29]. In December 1898, therefore, Harcourt also resigned, to be followed a month later by John Morley's retirement from the Liberal front bench. The removal from active politics of the irresolute trio of Rosebery, Harcourt and Morley, paved the way for the emergence of the dark horse, Henry Campbell-Bannerman, who in the end turned out to be a better political leader than all three. His election to the leadership in February 1899 begins a new period in the history of the Liberal Party.

These quarrels among the Liberal leaders were to some extent at least a reflection of deeper doubts and divisions within the party itself over policy, aims and tactics. What was the *raison d'être* of the Liberal Party in a post-Gladstonian world? That was the question that haunted the minds of Liberal politicians and publicists during these years.

In a notable study Professor Hamer has argued that the Victorian Liberal Party was essentially a coalition of disparate elements – nonconformists, trade unionists, temperance reformers, secularists, Home Rulers – united by no common ideology, each section demanding that priority and party support be given to its particular demands [44]. The Liberal leadership was therefore engaged in a continuous search for some formula that would introduce coherence and unity into a party which always threatened to degenerate into absolute chaos. Professor Hamer interprets the history of Victorian Liberalism in terms of a perpetual tension between two suggested solutions to this problem. On the one hand, the notion of 'the one great cause' – of which Irish Home Rule after 1886 is the outstanding example – which all sections of the party could accept as superior to their immediate and separate aims and unite around. On the other hand, 'programme politics', by which the Liberal Party would commit itself to a definite legislative programme embracing the formulae of all the Liberal sections but giving priority to none. The 'Newcastle Programme' of 1891 is the classical example of this type of commitment, though Irish Home Rule did inevitably head the list. In the development of this latter strategy Professor Hamer sees 1894 as a key date. He writes:

The sudden removal of the two factors which had disciplined and concentrated Liberal politics over the eight years since 1886 – Gladstone's leadership and the preoccupation with clearing the Irish 'obstruction' – restored to view the basic disorganisation of Liberal politics. Sectionalism re-emerged, rampant and uncontrollable. [44 *p. 185*]

It is this reversion to 'faddism', with each Liberal section pursuing its own hare oblivious of the rest of the field, that Hamer sees as one of the major sources of Liberal weakness in later Victorian England. Land reform, Welsh disestablishment, temperance reform, London 'progressivism', the 'rights of labour' – these were some of the fads taken up by Liberal factions during these years. 'Liberal Imperialism', the most intellectually distinguished of them all, began as an attempt to provide a new cohesive philosophy for the Liberal Party based on a commitment to 'national' rather than 'sectional' issues. Led by Lord Rosebery and supported by the brilliant trio of Asquith, Grey and Haldane, the Liberal Imperialists argued in favour of a combination of 'sane imperialism', 'national efficiency' and 'social welfare', all resting on the foundation of a stronger and more responsive State [61]. These ideas implied the notion of 'the clean slate', as Rosebery expressed it in his notorious speech at Chesterfield in December 1901; meaning, the downgrading in Liberal policy of unpopular and out-of-date shibboleths, notably Home Rule [64]. But the 'Liberal Imperialists' were and remained an elite, out of touch with grass-roots feeling – as their overzealous support for the Boer War showed – and in no position therefore to convert the party to their creed. 'Liberal Imperialism' too ended up as a section, a position which was formalised by the foundation of the Liberal League in 1902.

One should not exaggerate the debilitating consequences of sectionalism during this period. Some historians have argued (in opposition to Hamer) that sectionalism could be a source of strength as well as weakness for the Liberal Party. It helped to associate Liberalism with new, invigorating ideas and forces within late Victorian England, more particularly in relation to social questions and Celtic nationalism, and provided fresh channels for the flow of Liberal zeal and vitality. These years were the seed-bed of the 'New Liberalism' [24; 65].

If the problems of Liberal Party leadership and policy were worsened by the secession of 1886, so too was the more mundane problem of party organisation. This was a problem that was acute enough in any case owing to the electoral reforms of 1884 and 1885 – which increased the size of the electorate and the number of constituencies – and the democratisation of local government which followed the Acts of 1888 and 1894. But it was worsened by the exodus of men of wealth and influence from the ranks of the Liberal Party as a result of the Home Rule crisis. This meant that the whole work of local Liberal Associations in opposing the 'pull' of

Conservative influence, particularly in the rural areas, was jeopardised; and, in an age when members of parliament were unpaid and parliamentary candidates were still expected to contribute to election expenses, the Liberal Associations and the Central Office were faced with greater financial burdens and greater difficulties in finding suitable men. The result was, writes Halévy, that 'the party was obliged to be content with second rate candidates, cranks and men inspired by personal ambitions, political adventurers greedy of spoils and honours' [7 *p. 7*]. Halévy provides no details, but it is true that the sale of honours was, to some extent, deliberately increased by the Liberal government of 1892–95 [159]. What is quite clear, however, is that the Liberal Party now found it beyond its strength to contest every reasonable constituency in the country. Whereas up to 1886 there was no marked difference between the two parties in the number of unopposed seats, after that date the number of seats unopposed by the Liberals increased considerably. In 1895, for example, the Liberals allowed 114 Conservatives to be returned unopposed (compared with only 10 Liberals); in 1900 the figure was 138 (compared with 22 Liberals) [141]. It was only in 1906 that, as in so many other ways, the advantages of the two parties were reversed.

It is probable that the effects of the schism of 1886 on the fortunes of the Liberal Party have been exaggerated, especially as the National Liberal Federation remained loyal to Gladstone. For there is some evidence to suggest that there were long-term trends at work in the later nineteenth century which were in any case undermining the electoral strength of the party; though these, it must be admitted, are difficult to assess in detail since the constituency history of Great Britain during this period is, with a few notable exceptions, largely *terra incognita*.

One trend, however, which both historians and contemporary observers have commented on is the drift of the middle classes away from the Liberal towards the Conservative Party. This was a tendency which, as we saw earlier, could already be discerned in the election of 1868 and, even more impressively, in 1874, as a result of the whittling away of middle-class grievances by the great reforms of the mid-Victorian period, and the increasing identification of middle-class interests with those of the propertied classes generally, particularly in their suspicion of working-class demands [*Doc.* 6]. This meant that by 1880 the Liberals had largely lost suburbia; by 1885 the Conservatives had established a position of equality with the Liberals in the English boroughs; and thereafter the Liberal position worsened *vis-à-vis* the middle class as a result of the considerable advantage the Conservative Party gained by the establishment of single-member constituencies in 1885, and the events of 1886. As Professor Cornford puts it succinctly: 'With the extension of the suffrage class was becoming the most important single factor in deciding political allegiance' [94].

The problem for the Liberal Party in the 1890s, therefore, was to try to hold on to its middle-class supporters while increasing its support among the new working-class voters. This was particularly urgent for the party since the traditional nonconformist liberal bloc was a wasting asset, whereas working-class organisation and militancy – over one million members were enrolled in trade unions by 1893 – were rapidly increasing, and could be used perhaps to revitalise the Liberal Party. Unfortunately, during this decade the Liberal Party conspicuously failed to win over the urban working class, as Paul Thompson has shown in detail in the key area of Greater London. 'The loss of London', as he suggests, 'was as serious to the Liberals as that of Birmingham, and a major cause of the long Conservative ascendancy after 1886' [173 *p. 90*]. Nor did the Liberals fare much better in a mixed urban–rural area, as evidence from Northamptonshire seems to indicate [139].

Why then did the Liberal Party fail to increase its hold over the working class in the 1890s? Part of its failure was a failure of organisation; and money, as we have already seen, was at the heart of it. 'One of the chief causes of this want of proper organisation', wrote the Liberal Central Office, 'is the poverty of many of the constituencies . . . [where] the Liberal Party is composed of working men' [173 *p. 94*]. But the main answer lies in the failure of the Liberal Party to adapt itself to the needs of a new age. For by 1885–86 the major task of Gladstonian Liberalism, so far as the working class was concerned – the achievement of democratic rights – had been accomplished; the workers, both in town and country, now wanted more attention paid to their immediate bread-and butter needs in an age of rapid economic change, bitter industrial strife and widening social horizons [160]. The failure to recognise these aspirations, and to do for the Liberal Party what Disraeli had tried earlier to do for the Conservative Party, was partly a failure of Liberal leadership. Harcourt, despite his radical budgets, had little understanding of, or sympathy with, trade unionism [77]; Morley was dogmatically and defiantly a Gladstonian in social and economic affairs [43]; even Rosebery, who had built up something of a reputation as a social reformer while Chairman of the London

County Council, and who saw clearly enough the overwhelming need for the party to break away from the spell of Gladstone, lacked either the power or the will to do much about it. He was enough of an aristocrat in any case to be apprehensive about Harcourt's budget proposals, and to deprecate any attempt to turn the Liberals into a 'popular' party which 'would rest on nothing but a working-class support, without the variety and richness and intellectual forces which used to make up that party' [50 p. 342]. His government even failed to take seriously the party's proposal for the payment of members of Parliament. Rosebery's own interests as a minister lay, of course, primarily in foreign and imperial policy, but his own brand of Liberal Imperialism made a negligible appeal to working men, and could not in any case compete effectively with the dynamic creed of Joseph Chamberlain. Moreover, the personal feuds and hatreds of the men at the top largely vitiated any real attempt to reshape Liberal policy between 1894 and 1898. As the historian of their squabbles has written: their policies 'lacked coherence, consistency and a clearly defined aim. They wasted themselves in trivialities' [77 p. 173].

The failure of the Liberal Party to adopt policies which could appeal to workingmen was not wholly due to the Liberal leadership: the Liberal rank-and-file were also to blame. For another consequence of the secession of the Liberal Unionists in 1886 was to give the nonconformists and their Radical allies a greater say in the formation of the party's policies – and this had two important consequences. It meant, first, the adoption by the party of nonconformist fads – local option, disestablishment in Wales and Scotland – in which the workers had no real interest, and which helped to account for the defeat of 1895 [139]. It meant, secondly, that leading nonconformist employers – many of whom held key positions in the provincial party organisations – were often conspicuous for their anti-trade union attitudes and devotion to 'individualism' [42]. The suspicion of labour leaders for the Liberal Caucus was, therefore, often confirmed; and this was further reinforced by the refusal of many local Liberal Associations to countenance workingmen as parliamentary candidates, as in the classic case of Keir Hardie at Mid-Lanark in 1888 [Doc. 29]. The consequences of this were seen in the last five years of the nineteenth century. Then, on the one hand, the Liberal Party began to lose support to the right – to a Conservative Party, which, through its superior organisation and built-in advantages could exploit successfully the disunity, weaknesses and sectarianism of the

Liberals, and the grievances of the working class [130; 139]. But it also began to lose support to the Left: for since, in practice, the Liberal Party did so little for them, a new generation of labour leaders were now determined to assert their political independence more forcibly [169]. One way in which they could do this was by standing as Labour candidates in local elections, which they did with considerable success – at the expense of Liberalism – in areas like East London [173]. It is indeed the disastrous withering of the local roots of Liberalism during the 1890s that, for some historians, anticipates the national decline of the party in the twentieth century [173]. Another way in which they could assert their independence was by forming their own national party. The foundation of the Labour Party in 1900, therefore, is a fitting comment on the failures of the Liberal Party in the age of Rosebery and Harcourt.

5 CONSERVATIVE DOMINATION

CONSERVATIVES AND LIBERAL UNIONISTS

The long period of Conservative ascendancy at the end of the nineteenth century is associated peculiarly with the powerful figure of Lord Salisbury, Prime Minister for nearly fourteen years between 1885 and his retirement in 1902. It was Salisbury, therefore, rather than Disraeli, it has been suggested, who made the Conservative Party 'for the first time since Peel, a party of government' [86 pp. 244–5]. On becoming Prime Minister for the first time in June 1885 his major problem was the composition of the new ministry, and the clash of personalities among the contenders for office made it an especially delicate one. Two men were particularly important. On the one hand there was Sir Stafford Northcote who, despite the supine role he had played as Conservative Leader in the Commons in the previous five years, was a respected member of the party and a man of considerable ministerial experience: having been denied the highest post, he wished at the very least to continue as Leader in the Commons. On the other hand, there was Lord Randolph Churchill. Salisbury had already had one brush with him (as we saw earlier in our discussion of party organisation) over the National Union in 1883–84, and was acutely aware of the defects as well as the remarkable powers of this *enfant terrible* of the Conservative Party. Nevertheless, by 1885 Lord Randolph Churchill had proved himself the most formidable opponent of the Liberal government both inside and outside the House of Commons – and one of the few Conservatives who could arouse working-class audiences. To attempt to form a Conservative government 'without the man who is far and away the most popular Conservative in the House of Commons', as Hicks-Beach wrote to Salisbury, was an impossibility; and the Prime Minister perforce agreed [103 p. 176].

There was, however, one stumbling block – Churchill refused to serve under Northcote in the House of Commons. Since no

Conservative ministry could survive which did not contain both men, Salisbury had somehow or other to resolve their claims and those of their adherents, a task which was rendered particularly difficult by the vacillation of Northcote and the aloofness and arrogance of Churchill. For some days there was an impasse while recriminations mounted within the party. Eventually, as a result of the patience, good sense and insight of Salisbury, Northcote was 'kicked upstairs' as the Earl of Iddesleigh and made First Lord of the Treasury; Lord Randolph Churchill accepted the India Office, and his protagonist, Michael Hicks-Beach, became Leader in the Commons and Chancellor of the Exchequer. 'What a triumph!', wrote Chamberlain to Churchill. 'You have won all along the line' [103 *p. 191*]. Superficially this appeared to be true. Lord Randolph had won high office at an early age – he was only thirty-five – and with no ministerial experience; and the leader of the 'old gang' had been forced virtually to commit political suicide. But the real victor was once again, as in 1884, the man who had, with consummate skill, imposed his will on the members of the Conservative front bench and thereby consolidated his leadership of the party. 'The successful formation of his first ministry', writes R. R. James, 'was the first and possibly the most important of the triumphs in domestic politics achieved by Lord Salisbury' [103 *p. 189*].

The methods adopted by Churchill to push himself into office did little to endear him to the more orthodox members of the Conservative Party; they grumbled and waited. But from a strictly ministerial point of view he was an undoubted success at the India Office, and this fact, together with his brilliant onslaught on Gladstone's Home Rule policy in 1886, meant that he was bound to be considered for promotion when Lord Salisbury, after the Unionist success at the polls in the summer of that year, came to form his Second Ministry. Salisbury's doubts about Lord Randolph's temperamental fitness for Cabinet office and his suspicions of 'Tory Democracy' did not make him relish the prospect; nevertheless, once Hicks-Beach had insisted on yielding his place to him, there was no alternative but to appoint him Leader of the House and Chancellor of the Exchequer. 'He is very able', wrote Lord Cranbrook, 'but has he the balanced mind, the control of temper, the ready judgement, the knowledge of the House, of friends, of foes, which are requisite for a leader?' [103 *p. 250*]. Within a few months these doubts seemed to be confirmed. It was not only that Lord Randolph insisted on treating the Prime Minister as a political equal; nor was it just his promulgation of Tory Democracy to the country at large behind the back of the Cabinet – as in his notorious Dartford Speech in October 1886 – and his intimate political friendship with Joseph Chamberlain, still a dangerous Radical in the eyes of orthodox Conservatives. Rather it was, in Salisbury's own phrase, his 'incessant interference' and his attempt to impose his own policies on the Cabinet that was his most heinous offence; and this was particularly true of the Chancellor's brash attempts to influence the government's foreign policy – always Salisbury's first interest – now in the hands of his old opponent, Lord Iddesleigh.

By November Churchill was at odds with most of his colleagues over practically every aspect of policy – Ireland, local government, procedural reform as well as foreign affairs; and though Salisbury deferred to him as much as he could, his patience was wearing thin, as shown clearly in his letter to Cranbrook [*Doc. 30*]. It was at this point, as his daughter suggests, that Salisbury came to the conclusion that the point of no return had been reached in his relationship with Churchill: 'The experiment had failed . . . a breach was inevitable.' It is against this background of Salisbury's mounting irritation and Lord Randolph's increasing sense of isolation and frustration, that we must see the latter's famous 'resignation' letter of 20 December 1886, which was promptly accepted by the Prime Minister [103 *ch. x*].

The immediate result of Churchill's resignation was a political crisis owing to the difficulty of filling the posts he had vacated. 'I take a very dark view of our future', wrote Balfour, 'I think we must break up' [111 *p. 232*]. This could only be avoided, Salisbury believed, if the Liberal Unionists, who had given the government general support since its inception, now offered more positive help. It is at this point, therefore, that we may turn aside to consider the position of the small but vitally important group of Liberal Unionists led by that strange pair of bedfellows, Lord Hartington and Joseph Chamberlain.

The position of the Liberal Unionists after the general election of July 1886 depended on the simple fact that, partly as a result of their electoral pact with the Conservatives, they controlled seventy-eight votes in the House of Commons. This meant that the Conservative government under Lord Salisbury was indirectly dependent on their support, for, if they switched their votes to the official Liberal Party and the Irish, the government must collapse. In this anomalous situation lay at once the strength of the Liberal Unionist Party – since in return for their support they could hope to obtain 'liberal' concessions from their Conservative allies – but also their weakness, since, so long as the Liberal Party under Gladstone with its commitment to Home Rule was the greater evil, they would be prepared in the last resort to prop up a Conservative government whatever domestic policies it pursued, in order to maintain the Unionist front. The Liberal Unionists were in fact (like all third parties in British politics) in a cruel position. They had somehow or other, while giving general support to the Conservatives, to convince the country they were still *Liberals*, a confidence trick which in the end – as their connection with the parent party receded and the gravitational pull of the Conservative Party became more powerful – they found impossible to sustain. The point was put with admirable clarity by Joseph Chamberlain himself, writing to Hartington:

> Our great difficulty is that in order to preserve the Union we are forced to keep the Tory government in power. But every time we vote with them we give a shock to the ordinary Liberal politician outside, and if we do it too often, we shall be completely identified with the Tories and shall lose all chance of recovering the lead of the Liberal party. [41, ii *p. 268*]

The problem was even more complex and difficult than this indicates since the Liberal Unionists were not even a united party. In effect, they consisted of a large group of about fifty moderates or Whigs who looked to Hartington as their leader, and a smaller group of Radical unionists who followed Joseph Chamberlain; and the two leaders were now no more united over policy and tactics than they had been under Gladstone [124]. Hartington neither saw the position of the Liberal Unionists in quite the way that Chamberlain did, nor worried over it unduly. He was a Unionist first and foremost; and, never a great reformer even in his Gladstonian days, his attitude towards many of the problems of the day was now even less progressive than many members of the Conservative front bench. Having refused the premiership in July 1886 on the reasonable grounds that it would worsen the general Unionist position by driving many Liberals back to Gladstone, freed at last from the spur of the G.O.M.'s personal presence, and bound in any case soon to succeed to the duchy of Devonshire, both temperament and conviction made Hartington content on the whole to cede the initiative to the Conservative leaders and demand little in return. It was an attitude which infuriated Chamberlain. 'It is', as he kept reiterating to him, 'a purely negative policy' [32 *p. 275*]. But in any case Salisbury's magnanimous offer of agreeing to serve

under Hartington as Premier, and the fact that the latter controlled
the bulk of the Liberal Unionists, created a false impression of
Hartington's strength and that of his group. His passive leadership,
and the moderateness of his supporters – 'so moderate', as a
contemporary wrote, 'that a political microscope would have been
necessary to distinguish them from Conservatives born and bred'
[124 p. 72] – meant that they could provide the Conservative Party,
as Akers-Douglas, the Conservative Chief Whip, shrewdly noted,
with 'debating power in the House but outside their influence is
more likely to be a source of weakness than strength' [90 p. 104].
The moderates provided the shadow rather than the substance of
Liberal Unionist power.

   Far different was the position of Joseph Chamberlain. He had
taken great pains right from the start to dissociate his brand of
Unionism from that both of the Conservatives and the Whigs. He
had, for example, in June 1886 issued his own independent election
address, and in the same month formed the National Radical Union
(even though most of its members also joined the Liberal Unionist
Party); nor had he ever seriously considered the possibility of joining
a Conservative-dominated government. Chamberlain could afford to
be independent. For, unlike Hartington, his real power lay not in
Parliament, where he controlled only some twenty members, but, as
Michael Hurst has argued, in his electoral base in the Midlands: it
was the 'rock of regionalism' that sustained him [123]. His personal
control for the Unionist cause of the great bloc of constituencies in
and around Birmingham, made him both a local and a national
figure of importance – and a powerful independent force in his own
right. Though a passionate Unionist, Chamberlain intended, therefore, to use this power to push upon the Conservative government a
programme of reforms for Ireland and England, a policy which in
his eyes had not only political but tactical merits. For Chamberlain
had to prove that he was still a Liberal, not only to maintain the
devotion of his Midlands supporters, and prevent the drift of Liberal
Unionists – under the impact of Conservative reaction – back to the
old party, but to cover his own retreat if, as he still believed
possible, Gladstone retired, the Liberal Party dropped Home Rule,
and a reunited party looked around for a new leader. The policy he
tried to pursue, therefore, in the second half of 1886 was, as he
suggested to Hartington, 'never to vote with the Tories unless they
are in danger and to vote against them whenever we can safely do
so' [41, ii p. 268]. This was the attitude he adopted, though with
considerable difficulty, towards the Government's Irish policy, while

at the same time he tried to influence it, mainly through Lord Randolph Churchill, in the direction of more liberal policies generally.

It was this policy of vicarious Liberalism that seemed to be struck a vigorous blow by the resignation of Churchill in December 1886. 'I interpreted the event', wrote Chamberlain, 'as meaning that the reactionary party in the Cabinet had gained the upper hand' [40 p. 233. One important result of this was an attempt at Liberal reunion, on the initiative of Chamberlain and Harcourt, in the 'Round Table Conference' early in 1887. It was an odd episode. The bitterness between the two sides, the absence of Gladstone and Hartington – let alone the Irish – from the discussions, the continuance of mutual recriminations even while the conference was sitting, gave it an air of unreality and made its failure almost a foregone conclusion. In fact, it has been argued, in a detailed study by Michael Hurst, that Chamberlain's motives in supporting the conference were purely tactical. It was not a real attempt at reunion but a gesture towards his Birmingham supporters to show that his heart was still in the right place and that he had not gone over to the Conservatives unconditionally; just as he could argue once the conference was broken off that it was Gladstone, and not he, who was preventing reunion [125].

The resignation of Lord Randolph Churchill, however, as we have already seen, had another effect as far as the Liberal Unionists were concerned: it made the Conservatives more dependent on them for ministerial support. Indeed, Salisbury went so far as to offer the premiership once again to Hartington; but though he refused, for reasons similar to those that had moved him in July, he did strongly support the appointment of Goschen, the Liberal Unionists' financial expert, as Chancellor, although without committing the party as a whole. Goschen's appointment at the beginning of 1887, together with the unexpected choice of W. H. Smith as Leader of the House and A. J. Balfour as Irish Secretary (both as it turned out excellent appointments) ended successfully the political crisis that had faced Salisbury since the end of 1886.

Eighteen eighty-seven thus marks something of a turning point in the history of the Liberal Unionist Party, and its position after that date is described clearly by Joseph Chamberlain in his *Political Memoir* [Doc. 31]. For him too it was to be an important year. It seemed impossible to go back. 'I am reluctantly forced to the conclusion', he said at Birmingham in 1887, 'that the cleavage in the ranks of the Liberal Party has become complete and irretrievable'

[41, ii *p. 310*]; and it was hopeless to attempt to form a new party, especially as soon very few Liberal Associations were left to the Liberal Unionists. The only thing to do was to go forward – towards the Conservative Party, which at least offered the possibility of eventual office, and to a man of Chamberlain's energy and ability this was an important consideration. In 1887 he accepted from Lord Salisbury the leadership of a small delegation to the United States to discuss a fisheries dispute – a trivial incident, but the thin end of the wedge perhaps.

It was not just personal ambition, however, that made Chamberlain move inexorably towards the Conservative Party; changing political and economic circumstances were even more important. For if Chamberlain needed the Conservative Party, they also in a sense needed him: as a Midland political 'boss', and as a Radical who could act as a Unionist spokesman to the working class. A new *rapport* was now particularly urgent since the government's majority was steadily dropping, owing to the loss of by-elections to the Liberals. It was, therefore, bound to take more heed of the Chamberlainite reform programme, especially too as Churchill was now in the political wilderness. 'His influence accumulates though his party decays', wrote the parliamentary commentator, Henry Lucy, and Chamberlain was well aware of this [124 *p. 69*]. In 1889 he wrote to Hartington: 'We want to convince the country that there is a better chance of really popular reform from a Unionist Government than from the Parnell–Gladstone. It is true that certain great changes desired by many Liberals and by all Radicals are out of the question. Disestablishment is one of these' [124 *p. 91*].

Thus, though in the course of the next few years Chamberlain more or less abandoned his nonconformist past and the reform programme associated with it, he came to convince himself that the Salisbury ministry – with its reforms in local government, land-holding, Ireland, and education – was a genuine reformist government, introducing in fact much of his own 1885 'Unauthorised Programme'. It was these 'popular' reforms passed by a Conservative ministry under his influence, that he could now contrast with the irrelevant absurdities of the Liberal 'Newcastle Programme' of 1891, an attempt, as he said, 'to harmonise the political economy of Mr Tom Mann and Mr John Morley' [41, ii *p. 520*].

Though it would be false to denigrate Chamberlain's genuine and continuing interest in social reform during the years after 1887, it is clear nevertheless that his mind was turning more and more towards imperial affairs, and here his sympathies were even more with the policies of Lord Salisbury than they were with the 'Little Englandism' of the predominant section of the Liberal Party. In 1889 he strongly supported the government's retention of Egypt, and in the same year he visited the country and vigorously defended England's policies there in a speech at Birmingham in 1890. 'From that moment', says Garvin, 'he stood out as the leader of the new Imperialism' [41, ii *p. 456*], and Salisbury's work in Africa in the course of the next few years received his warm support. This new mutual respect between Chamberlain and the Conservative leaders was increased when, in 1891, Hartington retired to the Lords as the eighth Duke of Devonshire and Chamberlain became leader of the Liberal Unionists in the Commons, for he was able to establish particularly friendly relations with A. J. Balfour who became Conservative Leader there in the same year. Thus, symbolically, towards the end of 1891 Chamberlain sat side by side with Salisbury at a meeting in Birmingham of the Conservative National Union and declared the Unionist alliance 'indissoluble': 'Now', he said, referring to the Liberals, 'I neither look for nor desire reunion' [41, ii *p. 443*].

One last factor remained, that was finally to push Chamberlain and the Liberal Unionists towards a real alliance with the Conservative Party, and that was the record of the Liberal government between 1892 and 1895. It was not only that, for Chamberlain, the Liberals were tied indissolubly to the Irish Party and still committed to Home Rule; it was their attacks on the House of Lords which he particularly resented, for he saw them as an attempt to get round the fact that the English people had supported the Lords' rejection of the Second Home Rule Bill in 1893. But, at a more profound level, he also linked the 'new Liberalism' of the 'Newcastle Programme' and the attacks on the Lords with the growing menace of Socialism, a menace which was encouraged not only by these policies but by the weakness and disunity of the Liberal Party itself. A spectre was haunting England in the 1890s, in Chamberlain's imagination, the spectre of Socialism; and it was essential for all supporters of private property rights to sink their smaller differences in the face of this larger menace [*Doc. 32*]. Thus, as Peter Fraser writes, 'the socialist threat to property that emerged in the course of the Liberal ministries of 1892–95 provided just the tide of opinion that Chamberlain wanted to carry his party across the floor' [121 *p. 66*]. Hence in 1894 Chamberlain spoke on behalf of the Conservatives, and both sides began to think seriously about the implications of a Unionist victory at the next general election.

Chamberlain and the Liberal Unionists obtained from Salisbury much of what they wanted, and the sweeping Unionist victory in 1895 led Chamberlain, Devonshire and other Liberal Unionists to join Salisbury's Third Ministry, thus making it, in Ensor's phrase, 'one of the strongest that has ever held office in Great Britain' [5 *p. 224*]. The independent Liberal Unionist organisation, however, still remained, for as Chamberlain wrote somewhat petulantly to Devonshire: 'the rank and file in the country still maintain many of the old prejudices and will not join a Conservative party or Conservative organisation' [121]. The Unionist Party after 1895 was thus essentially a coalition, but a coalition united to defend not only the Union but propertied interests generally.

THE BASIS OF CONSERVATIVE POWER

Despite the remarkable change that took place in the leadership of the Conservative Party between the 1870s and the 1890s, there was little fundamental change in the character of the party or the nature of its support. The swing of the middle-class voter to the right which (as has been argued above) was typical of the age of Disraeli, was accelerated rather than halted in the age of the aristocratic Cecils; and, in particular, the leaders of financial and commercial wealth – formerly Liberal – were coming to find their natural resting place more and more in the party of Salisbury and Chamberlain. Ensor, in a much-quoted article, argued that the primary cause of this metamorphosis was Irish crime and violence – itself the consequence, fundamentally, of the agricultural depression which hit both Ireland and England after 1873 [157]. This view is really far too simple, for the changes in political allegiance which he discusses arose out of the general 'liberalisation' of mid-Victorian society and the rise of the working class. Nevertheless, Ensor does well to draw our attention to the importance of Irish affairs and agricultural depression in explaining the political displacements that occurred in the later nineteenth century. For if the Irish troubles of the 1880s did not cause, they at least stimulated the exodus of businessmen from the Liberal to the Conservative Party; and, as historians from Halévy onwards have noted, the Liberal Unionist Party which emerged as a result of the Home Rule crisis of 1886 was in a real sense the political expression of their economic power [7; 122].

The importance of the agricultural depression is perhaps even greater in considering the long-term development of the Conservative Party, for in the 1870s and 1880s it did help to undermine the economic position of at least an important section of the landed classes – the backbone of Conservatism – and thus revealed all too clearly their inability to pretend that they controlled any longer the real keys of political and administrative power. The decline of the landed interest in the later nineteenth century – psychological perhaps even more than economic – made it inevitable that the Conservative Party should accept for its own good the blood transfusion of energy, ability and, above all, wealth that the middle-class plutocracy could provide. In any case, as F. M. L. Thompson has shown, the distinction between 'landed' and 'commercial' wealth was rapidly becoming a myth, at least for the upper echelons of landed society, whose members, like the Dukes of Devonshire and Northumberland, and even Salisbury himself, were now investing widely in industrial and railway shares and commercial ventures overseas [162]. After 1886, therefore, the Conservative Party was well on the way to becoming the party of the landed and financial plutocracy, and mainly responsible for that 'atmosphere of money in the lobby of the House of Commons' that the *Economist* found so reprehensible in 1899 [7 *p. 17*]. From this point of view, too, the political alliance of 1895 between the Conservative and Liberal Unionist Parties was merely the parliamentary expression of an economic and social *fait accompli* which had been building up during the previous thirty years.

The Conservative Party in the later years of the nineteenth century, therefore, was no longer dominated completely by the ethos of the landed classes (with whom may be associated the Church of England), but by the interests of the propertied classes generally, and this is reflected to some extent in the composition of both houses of Parliament. Here, as in so many other ways, the year 1885 is something of a turning point. For after the general election of that year for the first time members of the industrial and commercial interest outnumbered members of the landed interest in the House of Commons. This was, of course, merely the middle class coming belatedly into its parliamentary inheritance, as Bagehot had already noted in 1872 in one of the most famous sections of his *English Constitution* [15 *p. 274*]. But since the Liberal Party had always had more commercial men in its ranks than the Tories, it is the changes in the parliamentary composition of the Conservative Party after that date that are the more remarkable, though these, it must be admitted, are difficult to assess precisely, owing to the problems of defining the different 'groups'. But in 1868, according to the figures of W. L. Guttsman, 46 per cent of Conservative MPs belonged to the landed interest; 31 per cent came from commerce and industry; and 9 per cent belonged to the professions. In 1885 the figures for these three groups were 23 per cent, 50 per cent and 16 per cent respectively; and in 1900 (including Liberal Unionists) 20, 52 and 18 per cent [158 *p. 104*]. This would indicate a fairly rapid fall in the numbers belonging to the landed interest (but see [95]).

Another, slighter, indication of the change in the character of the Conservative Party can be seen in the membership of the Upper House. 'Tradition, personal merit, and Bagehot's plutocracy made terms with one another', writes F. M. L. Thompson, 'and nowhere is this more visible than in the history of the peerage after 1885' [162 *p. 292*]. The number of peerages themselves rose after that date; but what is more significant is the increasing ennoblement of those with commercial and industrial backgrounds. In the ten years before 1886 only four such peerages had been created; in the ten years after 1886 there were eighteen; and in the whole period from 1886 to 1914 out of the 200 or so men who then entered the peerage for the first time, more than one-third were industrialists and less than a quarter were members of landed families [159; 162]. The turning point in this process, writes its historian, 'appears to have been . . . the first Salisbury ministry in 1885–86' when 'for the first time, and always thereafter, 20 per cent or more of all recipients had (commercial and industrial) connections' [161 *p. 8*]; a tribute in itself to the Prime Minister's recognition of party needs. One other indication perhaps of the changing nature of the Conservative Party is the rise of the Fair Trade Movement after 1881 and its close links with the party. It is true, of course, that a section of the farmers (though not the greater landowners) strongly supported the movement and reflected, therefore, the traditional link between the Conservative Party and the land. But, as the historian of the Fair Trade League suggests, the spread of its ideas 'was largely the work of manufacturers who suffered from foreign competition and foreign tariffs' [156 *p. 1*]; and the fact, therefore, that at least six members of Salisbury's government in 1886 spoke favourably of its ideas, and that the Conservative National Union in 1887 and 1891 carried protectionist motions, is an indication now of the party's increasing concern for the interests of trade and industry rather than of agriculture. It reveals too the key importance of the views of the small group of Conservative members who sat for industrial constituencies in Sheffield, Bradford, and elsewhere, where industry was hard hit by increasing competition from abroad.

It would be completely false to assume, however, that these changes in the composition of the Parliamentary Conservative Party were reflected proportionately in its leadership. In fact, as is clear purely from *prima facie* evidence, the leaders of Conservative governments and the party machine were still mainly aristocratic or associated with the landed interest: what is more remarkable, therefore, about the Conservative Party in the later nineteenth century is not the decline of the landed interest in terms of wealth and numbers, which was inevitable, but the tenacity and relative ease with which it was able to cling to its over-representation in every aspect of party life. This was, of course, a tribute to the ability of a Salisbury, an Akers-Douglas or an A. J. Balfour, but, Cornford adds, ability decided 'only which aristocrats should dominate the party' [95 p. 270]. How far this was an electoral asset in an age when, Halévy suggests, the peerage was particularly popular, is difficult to determine [7 p. 22]. But what does seem beyond dispute is that the partnership of wealth *and* title within the ranks of the Unionist Party did give it considerable advantages. It helps to explain the success of Conservative organisation compared with the Liberals; for it was money that helped to oil the wheels of the efficient party machine controlled by Akers-Douglas and Captain Middleton and enabled them, for example, to employ thirty party agents in the London area to the Liberals' three [173 p. 110]. This was particularly important in the great cities where the Conservative Party was appealing successfully to the working classes. In the rural areas such overt organisation was hardly necessary. The county elite of farmers, gentry and Anglican clergy – stolidly Unionist after 1886, and still dominating the bench and local government – exercised a real, though unacknowledged, 'pull' over the local voters in favour of the Conservative Party, and made the task of the Liberal worker in most country constituencies particularly heartbreaking [131; 133].

The Conservative Party also gained from the inbuilt advantages that the electoral system itself gave to owners of property. For, contrary to popular belief, the electoral legislation of the 1880s did not, as Charles Seymour pointed out half a century ago, introduce 'a completely democratic system', even apart from the obvious fact that women did not possess the vote [150 p. 156]; and in his detailed study of the franchise system between 1885 and 1918 Neal Blewett has shown that something like 40 per cent of adult males did not exercise the vote [127]. Why was this? Some men were in fact specifically excluded from the franchise: domestic servants, policemen and soldiers living in barracks, and – particularly resented – those on poor relief. But even more damning was the fact that about half of those who were not on the electoral register in 1911 were excluded, not because they lacked the necessary franchise qualifications, but through the workings of the archaic registration system, with its insistence, for example, on twelve months' possession to exercise the household franchise. Many of the members of this great army of the disenfranchised-in-practice – about one million men annually – were workingmen, often changing jobs, and it is impossible to tell exactly how they would have voted after 1885 if given the chance. But, by contrast, if the poor often lost the vote, the rich often gained votes owing to the practice by which owners of businesses and university graduates were given votes additional to the ones they exercised in their home constituencies. Such plural votes, it has been estimated, amounted (in 1911) to some 7 per cent of the total electorate [127]; and though we may discount the wilder claims made by opposition spokesmen in the 1890s in denouncing the system of plural voting, both Seymour and Blewett conclude that it did produce some bias in favour of the Unionists.

They gained even more from the Redistribution Act of 1885 which they insisted – owing to the successful Conservative blackmailing tactics in the House of Lords – should accompany the Reform Act of the previous year [140], for the Conservative Party was alarmed lest the considerable increase in votes produced by that Act – the number of voters rose from about 900,000 to 2.5 million in the counties – should, if unaccompanied by redistribution, swamp the old constituencies and produce an overwhelming swing to the left. Hence, paradoxically, the Conservative leadership was prepared to support a radical redistribution measure which would sacrifice the small boroughs in favour of an almost universal division of the country into one-member constituencies, believing that, however the rural labourer voted, the Conservative Party would still make great gains in the cities. 'I believe there is', commented Salisbury, 'a great deal of villa Toryism which requires organisation' [85 *p. 154*]. Roughly speaking that is what did happen. The abolition or reduction of the representation of the smaller boroughs by the 1885 Act made 142 seats available for redistribution: sixty-eight were given to the English and Welsh counties, but seventy-four went to the boroughs, with the great provincial cities gaining three to six more members and Greater London gaining another thirty-nine [150]. The country was at the same time divided up into constituencies roughly equal in population, and the parliamentary map of Great Britain, which had existed without fundamental change for some three centuries, finally disappeared, unmourned [128]. The position in the cities was now vital. They were carved up deliberately on largely 'class' lines, and the importance of this fact for the Conservative Party is put succinctly by Professor Cornford: 'Where Conservative supporters had formerly been swamped in huge constituencies, they were now high and dry on islands of their own' [94]. The result of this was seen in 1885 when, for the first time, the Conservatives won a majority in the English boroughs. Indeed, the pattern laid down in that election – when Conservative strength was concentrated in London, Lancashire, the non-industrial counties, and the smallest and largest of the boroughs – was to be roughly repeated in the next five elections [94].

So far we have considered certain general advantages possessed by the Conservative Party in the later nineteenth century. What, however, was the role of Conservative leadership and policy in accounting for the party's long period of domination? Lord Salisbury, who led the Conservative Party during the years between 1885 and 1902, was in some ways, despite his outstanding qualities as a statesman, an odd person to be party leader during this period [85; 114]. He himself, as he said, lacked 'the gifts of pliancy and optimism' [88, iii *p. 110*] which he believed the leader of a great party must possess, and his agility of mind, mordant wit, and political cynicism, were often disconcerting to his slower colleagues. 'He was' as Paul Smith suggests, 'one of those untypical and sometimes uncongenial figures, like Peel, or Disraeli, or Churchill, by whom the Conservative party allows itself to be led from time to time, because it needs the qualities of intellect, or imagination, or character which they can supply' [113 *intro.*].

In a profound sense he was never really a politician in the way that Disraeli was, just as he totally lacked his predecessor's flair for publicity; but, though he despised such things, he did what was required of him by way of dispensing patronage and stumping the country. Indeed, he has been described as 'an astute and often devastatingly skilful general, in domestic party warfare' [106 *pp. 2–3*]. He ran the Cabinet on a very loose reign, and much preferred the Foreign Office to being Prime Minister, a post which, he remarked, conferred 'no real power' [88, iii *p. 111*]. At the Foreign Office, of course, his work was outstanding; in domestic affairs, however, he possessed, suggests A. J. P. Taylor, 'the outlook of a slow-witted countryman' [14 p. 122]. This is perhaps going a bit far, though Salisbury would have relished the remark. But certainly the Prime Minister's brand of Conservatism, with its emphasis on the need for individual effort and strong government and its barely concealed distaste for state activity, democracy and progress, seemed to belong to a bygone age [117]. 'I reckon myself', he wrote, 'as no higher in the state of things than a policeman – whose utility would be gone if the workers of mischief disappeared' [88, iii p. 147]. He tended perhaps to see 'workers of mischief' all around him on the domestic front in the 1890s, and his correspondence is full of gloomy forebodings for the future. Such an outlook, together with a penchant for giving jobs to his relatives, led to grumblings from those more progressive Conservative members – such as J. A. Gorst or G. C. T. Bartley – who felt that they were outside the magic circle [Doc. 33]. But Salisbury's power, in a strictly party sense, rested securely on the support of the landed classes, and on the lucky fact that, on the outstanding issues of the day – Ireland, Socialism, foreign and imperial policy – his views coincided with those of the overwhelming majority of Conservative members. His nephew and successor, A. J. Balfour, was not to be so lucky.

It was hardly to be expected then that Salisbury would prove to be a great reformer. 'He was', writes his daughter, 'by temperament and opinion incapable of becoming a great law-maker. He did not believe in any good to be affected by "inspired" ventures in legislation' [88, iii p. 167]. He was not averse to some aspects of reform, as in housing or local government, and, as he observed cynically of the County Councils Bill of 1888, it was in the fashion, and 'against fashion it is almost impossible to argue' [107 p. 142]. But his attitude towards reform was conditioned less by his personal predilections, than by his understanding of the character of the Conservative Party, the pulls and pressures of groups, interests and individuals within it, and the situation in which it found itself after 1886; in all of which he was powerfully helped by the support and advice of Akers-Douglas and Captain Middleton, Chief Whip and party agent. For, in the first place, Lord Salisbury was conscious – over-conscious some loyal supporters believed in 1886 – of the vital importance of Liberal Unionist support, and was realistic enough to realise that some reform was needed to placate it. 'It is the price we have to pay for the Union', he wrote of the Irish Land Bill of 1887, 'and it is a heavy one' [97 pp. 239–40]. But it was a price he was always prepared to pay [96]. As Peter Marsh argues, 'Opposition to

Home Rule was the keystone of Salisbury's power', and it is this that helps to explain also his strong support for Balfour's tough policy in Ireland during the years of his Secretaryship, and his hounding of Parnell over the 'Times Forgeries' in 1887 [106 p. 155].

Part of that price also, more negatively, was the inability of the party to abandon Free Trade in the 1880s and early 1890s, and it is his awareness of that basic limitation that explains Salisbury's hedging over the issue when confronted with the protectionist sentiments of the Conservative National Union [156]. Quite apart from the alliance with the Liberal Unionists, however, as Cornford observes, 'the Conservative party itself was a coalition, both socially and politically' [95 p. 306]. This meant that the Prime Minister had to face pressure also from the 'reformist' group of MPs within the party, many of whom sat for industrial constituencies and who were, therefore, forced to push the interests of their working-class constituents. It was these men who, as we have seen, often supported the protectionist movements of the period, and it was they also who were most sympathetic to the Chamberlainite proposals for social reform, like the scheme for old age pensions.

For a variety of reasons, then, Salisbury was willing to accept a number of reforms, some of which went against the grain, and on occasion he was prepared to use blackmail tactics to impose them upon his recalcitrant right wing. But there was a limit to what he could or would do, and that limit was set, he believed, and as he pointed out in a remarkable letter to Lord Randolph Churchill, by the attitudes of 'the classes and the dependants of class', the country gentlemen and their supporters [Doc. 34]. For in Salisbury's eyes they still formed the most important section of the Conservative Party: the most stable, the most worthy and the most loyal, and indeed the group with whom his real sympathies lay. It was their interests, their prejudices even, that must be taken into account when considering the programme of the party. Not that he did much for them positively. 'They will not find – they cannot find', he wrote, in reference to the agricultural depression, 'in the doctrines of protection any alleviation from the ruin which in too many instances threatens them' [88, iv p. 180–1]. But it was of them he was probably thinking when he wrote of the Conservative Party in a valedictory letter to Alfred Milner:

It is a party shackled by tradition; all the cautious people, all the timid, all the unimaginative, belong to it. It stumbles slowly and painfully from precedent to precedent with its eyes fixed on the ground. Yet the Conservative Party is the Imperial Party. I must work with it – who indeed am just such an one myself . . . . [97 *p. 252*]

Conservative reform legislation (or lack of it) was often the outcome of subtle and detailed negotiations and conflict within the party. But when all is said and done it cannot be maintained that the party's record was very impressive during the fourteen or so years of Salisbury's rule. One great Act – the County Councils Act of 1888 – and a few minor ones were passed during his Second Ministry between 1886 and 1892; after 1895, even with Chamberlain and the Liberal Unionists in the government, the record was even thinner; and over the whole period of Salisbury's ascendancy practically nothing was done to improve the condition of life of the working classes. Why was this? And why was the Conservative Party able to maintain itself in power during this long period?

The orthodox answer usually given by historians is that the masses were beguiled by imperialism. Professor Beer, in his book on *Modern British Politics*, puts the argument quite unequivocally. The lack of social reform, he writes, 'is most readily explained on simple electoral grounds. In imperialism (including in this not only the question of Empire but also of union with Ireland) the party had found a cause with a mighty appeal to the electorate' [126 *p. 272*]. But if the general trend of much recent research on later nineteenth-century political history has been, by implication, to cast doubt on the view that (except in special areas like Lancashire) the working-class electorate was vitally influenced by the Home Rule issue, the same point has been made by Henry Pelling about imperialism proper. 'There is no evidence', he writes, 'of a direct continuous support for the cause of Imperialism among any section of the working class' [170 *p. 99*]. The rhetoric of imperialism in its Kiplingesque aspect, he argues, never appealed to the working class at all. The only election during this period where imperial sentiment played a part was the notorious 'Khaki Election' of 1900, where it probably helped to stave off a Liberal victory (the government's majority had been falling rapidly), though even there he stresses the importance of social and economic factors. In 1895, where Ensor sees the Unionist victory as due primarily to the force of 'expansive imperialism', Pelling emphasises economic factors and the unpopularity of Liberal policies [5; 170].

Pelling's views have been reinforced by Richard Price's detailed study of the working class and the Boer War, based on evidence mainly from the workingmen's clubs. He too finds an absence of jingoism, almost an indifference to the war, and indeed the existence in an inchoate and unorganised fashion of strong anti-war feeling [171]. Imperialism for the working class was primarily important from the point of view of jobs and wages; and (as Pelling argues elsewhere) they were not in any case much interested in social reform *per se* – that was the prerogative of middle-class do gooders [170 *ch. 1*]. Perhaps, therefore, this 'jobs' aspect of imperialism did have some effect during the later 1890s: not Salisbury's view that the scramble for Africa was 'a great civilising, Christianising force' [88, iv *p. 310*] but rather his argument that 'to keep our trade, our industries alive we must open new sources of consumption in the more untrodden portions of the earth' [107 *p. 106*]. But certainly, whatever its effect on the working class, such an appeal was bound to tie the forces of industrial and commercial wealth ever more closely to the Conservative Party.

Two general conclusions may, therefore, be tentatively suggested to account for Conservative domination in the later nineteenth century. First, it was not so much that the mass of voters were attracted positively to Conservative policies and politicians, but rather that they reacted against the weaknesses of contemporary Liberalism. This is linked to some extent with the 'lull' in political fervour that Professor Hanham notes as characteristic of this period [136 *p. 27*], and is shown in working-class abstentions at the polls. Richard Shannon has recently argued, however, that many members of the new middle classes – created by the expansion of commerce, finance, and the service industries – deliberately supported the Conservative Party, as the party which opposed the encroaching power of the state and the pretensions of industrial trade unionism. It was Salisbury's party which was thus prepared 'to fight . . . the political war of the consumers against the producers' [111 *p. 556*]. Secondly, working-class voters were concerned primarily with bread-and-butter issues – jobs, wages, prices – often seen within a specifically local context, as with the problem of immigration in East London at the end of this period [149; 173]. It was the link between these issues and their 'image' of the parties, that explained how and whether they voted.

PART THREE: ASSESSMENT

At the death of Queen Victoria in 1901 the British party system was already beginning to assume the shape that it was to retain until at least the outbreak of the Second World War. The Conservative Party, as a result of the developments in the later nineteenth century that have already been discussed, had, by that date, managed to build up a firm electoral base by winning the allegiance of the bulk of the middle class, and obtaining normally about one-third of the working-class vote. It was the ability of the Conservative Party to gain the support of such a large section of the working class that has enabled it since 1885 to win a clear majority of the general elections that have been held, and thus to exhibit, in the words of McKenzie and Silver, 'a record of electoral success almost unrivalled among political parties in parliamentary systems' [167 *p. 10*]. Yet, curiously, the Conservative Party in 1901, though dependent on mass support, was led by that epitome of the old aristocratic ruling class, the Marquis of Salisbury; and, after Salisbury's retirement in 1902, he was succeeded for another nine years by another Cecil, his nephew, A. J. Balfour.

Yet appearances are deceptive. The political foundations of the 'Hotel Cecil' were being undermined well before Balfour was forced to retire as leader of the party in 1911. For in a party which was becoming increasingly dominated financially, and at the parliamentary level, by businessmen, it was impossible to stave off for ever the evil day when they would demand some return, in terms of real leadership, for their support. Deference might still be shown to the aristocracy, but that deference was now based not on blood and title but on political skill and success. And those were the very things that Balfour was unable to provide. The ease with which he had slipped into the premiership in 1902, after his uncle's retirement, was a tribute not so much to Balfour's family name, as to the ability he had displayed earlier as Irish Secretary and Leader of the Commons. Unfortunately, his behaviour after that date showed that he lacked the qualities of firmness and decisiveness necessary in a Prime Minister, and possessed, moreover, an olympian insensitiveness to powerful currents of opinion both in the country – as shown by his egregious blunder over 'Chinese slavery' – and indeed within his own party, though this was partly due to the tameness of the National Union. Hence within eighteen months of becoming Prime Minister Balfour was faced with a crisis over tariff reform precipitated by Joseph Chamberlain, and, though he desperately tried to maintain his own supremacy and heal the fissures in the party, he eventually gave up the attempt and resigned as Prime Minister in 1905 [41 v, vi]. The colossal electoral disaster of 1906, together with – as many Conservative back-benchers came to feel – his subsequent puerile leadership during the constitutional crises of 1909–11, led to a 'Balfour must go' movement, and in November 1911 he resigned as leader of the Conservative Party.

The replacement of Balfour by Bonar Law, the Scots-Canadian ironmaster, seemed to symbolise the coming to power within the party of the new type of Conservative industrialist. Law's successors, Baldwin and Neville Chamberlain, were men of much the same stamp; and the Conservative Party in the interwar years, therefore, seemed to be dominated by those 'hard-faced businessmen' who had begun to enter the party in the age of Disraeli. Nor did the change in the character of its leadership have any profound effect on the party's electoral position. It was the Conservative Party that gained most from the wartime coalition and the subsequent 'Coupon Election' of 1918; but the country was in any case moving to the right, and Conservative or Conservative-dominated governments were characteristic of the interwar period.

Far different was the position of the Liberal Party. It is true that after a long period of decline in the later years of the nineteenth century, the Liberal Party made a remarkable recovery in the early years of the new century and won a landslide victory in the 1906 general election, gaining 400 seats and an overall majority in the House of Commons of 130. That victory was mainly due, Peter Clarke argues, to strong support from the industrial working classes for the social and economic policies associated with the 'New Liberalism' [33]. The outstanding social reforms that were then introduced by the Liberals – especially old-age pensions and the insurance legislation of 1911 – are generally considered to be the most important part of their domestic programme, and appear to mark a break with Victorian attitudes towards the role of the state in the social field. What is also noteworthy, however, is the remarkable continuity in other aspects of domestic policy between the governments of Campbell-Bannerman and Asquith (both of whom served in Gladstone's Fourth Ministry, 1892–94) and later Victorian Liberalism [1 *ch.* 8]. Progressive tax policies, land reform, the limiting of the constitutional powers of the House of Lords in 1911, and, above all, the Third Home Rule Bill of 1912 (which was virtually a replica of Gladstone's 1893 Bill), all this had already been outlined in the Liberals' Newcastle Programme of 1891.

The great ministry of Asquith, Lloyd George and Churchill, which lasted from 1908 to 1915, proved, however, to be England's 'last Liberal government'. Signs of Liberal weakness were already apparent before the First World War. In the general elections of 1910 the Liberals lost more than 100 seats (mainly due to the defection of the middle classes) and were reduced to exactly the same total as the Conservatives in the House of Commons; only support from Labour and the Irish enabled them to continue as the governing party. Moreover, between 1910 and 1914 the Liberal Party lost a further fifteen seats to the Tories. During these years the Liberals were also faced with the new and politically more dangerous rivalry of the Labour Party, founded in 1900, at the very end of our period; and Labour's *raison d'être* was to win over the working-class vote [164].

Since, however, the Liberal Party was able to contain the Labour Party, electorally and ideologically, during this prewar period, a number of historians have pointed to the First World War as the key factor that led to the decline of the Liberal Party [23]. The war resulted in the passage of the Reform Act of 1918 which, by removing most of the technical restrictions on the exercise of the franchise and granting the vote to women over the age of thirty, created for the first time a mass, democratic electorate. In facing the challenge of Labour for the allegiance of the working-class electorate in the postwar world, the Liberals were now at a clear disadvantage. For they were divided between the supporters of Asquith and those of Lloyd George; and even after they were reunited in an uneasy alliance after 1923, under the leadership of Asquith, the Asquithians had no new policies to offer the nation, and the Liberal Party was racked by organisational and financial difficulties. By contrast, the Labour Party emerged from the First World War united and confident, with a new national organisation and programme, and ample funds and strong support from a powerful and expanding trade union movement [168]. In Ramsay

MacDonald too they soon had an outstanding party leader, and MacDonald's immediate aim was the destruction of the Liberal Party as a potential party of government. In this he was completely successful. By 1924, after the general election of that year, the Liberal Party – with only forty MPs in the Commons – had been pushed definitely into third place in the electoral stakes, a position which was confirmed by the subsequent general elections of the interwar period and underlined by Labour's massive victory in 1945. Once the great party of Gladstone, the Liberal Party was now a party on the margin of politics. It is these developments that mark the most profound transformation in the British party system compared with the later Victorian period.

PART FOUR: DOCUMENTS

DOCUMENT 1   THE NONCONFORMISTS AND THE
LIBERAL PARTY

*The nonconformist community normally formed the most loyal bloc of
voting support for the Liberal Party in the nineteenth century [but see Doc.
4]. The following extract well illustrates the reasons for this, and indicates
also the 'tone' of much nonconformist writing on political affairs.*

Since the beginning of the century . . . it is certain that Britain has, in the
intervals of her blindness, had some inspiring visions of the kingdom of
justice one day to be established among men, and it is not to be denied that,
taken broadly, the Liberal Party has striven to follow the fiery pillar of
conscience into this promised land . . . speaking generally it has striven to
be 'the party of Christ' . . . the party of moral principles as against that of
selfish and corrupt interests, the party of peace as against that of violence,
the party of popular improvement and reform as against that of resistance
to progress, the party of justice as against that of despotic force or social
disorder . . . . The strength of the Liberal Party is, and always has been, in
the force of individual and social conscience.

From the *Nonconformist*, 1 January 1880. Quoted in Glaser, [42].

DOCUMENT 2   GLADSTONE AND THE MASSES

*Gladstone's Midlothian Campaign 1879–80 marked his re-entry into active
politics, and was a bitter attack on Disraeli's foreign and imperial policies.
The following extract shows why he was revered by the working people and
distrusted by the upper classes.*

We have great forces arrayed against us . . . . I am sorry to say we cannot
reckon upon what is called the landed interest, we cannot reckon upon the
clergy of the established church either in England or Scotland . . . . On
none of these can we place our trust. We cannot reckon on the wealth of
the country, nor upon the rank of the country, nor upon the influence
which rank and wealth usually bring. In the main these powers are against

us, for wherever there is a close corporation, wherever there is a spirit of organised monopoly, wherever there is a narrow and sectional interest apart from that of the country, and desiring to be set up above the interest of the public, there, gentlemen, we, the liberal party, have no friendship and no tolerance to expect. Above all these, and behind all these, there is something greater than these – there is the nation itself.

Speech at West Calder, 1 April 1880. Quoted in Morley, [66], ii, p. 218.

DOCUMENT 3   A CONSERVATIVE VIEW OF THE GOVERNMENT, 1873

Northcote, like many leading Conservatives, supported Disraeli's refusal to take office in 1873 after Gladstone's temporary retirement. His letter reveals a remarkable understanding of the currents of opinion at work in the country.

But looking at the matter broadly, and in the interest of the Conservative cause as distinct from that of the present representatives of the Conservative party, I am strongly convinced that time is required to mature the fast ripening Conservatism of the country, and to dispel the hallucinations which have attached a great mass of moderate men to the Liberal cause. I believe that the disintegration of Gladstone's party has begun and that nothing but precipitancy on our part can arrest it. He has expended the impetuous force which brought him into office, and now is brought face to face with new, or rather old, difficulties which he can hardly surmount without alienating one or the other wing of his party. If he goes on with the Extreme section, a large body of his moderate supporters will rank themselves with the Conservatives, if he quarrels with the Extreme section they will become the Opposition, while the conduct of affairs will fall to the acknowledged Conservatives, who will obtain the support of the moderate Liberals. But if we appeal to the country before the breach in the Liberal ranks is fully made, and before the policy of the Extreme men is fully developed, we shall consolidate them; the Extreme men will hold back a little and the moderate advance a little and there will be more confusion and confiscation.

Sir Stafford Northcote to Disraeli, 14 March 1873. Quoted in Feuchtwanger, [133], p. 14.

DOCUMENT 4   THE NONCONFORMIST REVOLT

R. W. Dale was a Congregational minister and one of the leaders of the campaign against the Liberal government's education policy.

They have deliberately chosen to pursue a retrograde policy, and although we have cherished a hearty loyalty to the old leaders of the Liberal Party, our loyalty to the principles which both they and we are called to defend is stronger, more intense, deeper than loyalty to them. We are at last thrown upon ourselves; for a time, perhaps, for a few years, we shall have to act independently of the recognised leaders of the Liberal party. The old union between them and us is now dissolved. I do not regard that dissolution with any degree of satisfaction.

From R. W. Dale, *The Elementary Education Act (1870) Amendment Bill and the Political Policy of Nonconformists,* Birmingham, 1873.

DOCUMENT 5   THE DECLINE OF GLADSTONE'S FIRST
                        MINISTRY

Faced with opposition from nonconformists and workingmen over his Trade Union and Education Acts, and with weakness and disunity within the Cabinet, Gladstone hints at a dissolution and a new general election.

The signs of weakness multiply, and for some time have multiplied, upon the government, in the loss of control over the legislative action of the House of Lords, the diminution of the majority in the House of Commons without its natural compensation in increase of unity and discipline, and the almost unbroken series of defeats at single elections in the country. In truth the government is approaching, though I will not say it has yet reached, the condition in which it will have ceased to possess that amount of power which is necessary for the dignity of the crown and the welfare of the country; and in which it might be a godsend if some perfectly honourable difference of opinion among ourselves on a question requiring immediate action were to arise, and to take such a course as to release us collectively from the responsibilities of office ... the nation appears to think that it has had enough of us. ... It is a question of measures then: can we by any measures materially mend the position of the party for an impending election?

Gladstone to Lord Granville, 8 January 1874. Quoted in Morley, [66], ii, pp. 89–90.

DOCUMENT 6   THE GENERAL ELECTION OF 1874

Frederic Harrison was a Radical, a Positivist and a shrewd political analyst, as the following extract shows. The Fortnightly Review was the leading highbrow Radical journal of the mid-Victorian period, edited then by John Morley.

The real truth is that the middle-class, or its effective strength, has swung round to Conservatism. Conservatism no doubt it is of a vague and negative kind; but its practical effect is an undefined preference for 'leaving well alone'. When we look at the poll in the City of London, in Westminster, in Middlesex, in Surrey, in Liverpool, Manchester, Leeds and Sheffield, in the metropolitan boroughs and in the home counties, in all the centres of middle-class industry, wealth and cultivation, we see one unmistakeable fact, that the rich trading-class, and the comfortable middle-class has grown distinctly Conservative. There are no special causes at work in these great constituencies. Beer has no influence with the merchants, shopkeepers and citizens of London. There are no dockyards in Surrey and Middlesex. There are no great landlords or employers in Marylebone. The Carlton Club cannot pull the wires of Manchester and Sheffield. The 25th Section men are not very strong in Westminster, and there is no 'residuum' in Hertfordshire and Essex, in Lancashire and Yorkshire counties. These great boroughs and counties contain the very flower of the men of business, whose indomitable energy builds up these five millions of surplus, who pay so large a proportion of that income-tax which was offered them as a bonus. The inference is unmistakeable. The effective force of the middle-class has grown for a season Conservative. The Conservative party has become as much the middle-class party as the Liberal used to be, as much and more.

The sleek citizens, who pour forth daily from thousands and thousands of smug villas round London, Manchester and Liverpool, read their Standard and believe that the country will do very well as it is . . . . Conservatism has opened its arms to the middle-classes, and has reaped its just reward. . .

This, then, appears to us the great lesson of the elections of 1874, that the middle-classes have gone over to the enemy bag and baggage.

From Frederic Harrison, 'The Conservative Reaction', *The Fortnightly Review*, vol. 15, 1874.

DOCUMENT 7   ENGELS ON THE GENERAL ELECTION OF 1868

Engels had a considerable knowledge of English economic and political conditions. Like Marx, however, he was continually disillusioned by the unrevolutionary behaviour of English workingmen.

What do you say to the elections in the factory districts? Once again the proletariat has discredited itself terribly. Everywhere the proletariat is the tag, rag and bobtail of the official parties, and if any party has gained strength from the new votes it is the Tories . . . it remains a disastrous certificate of poverty for the English proletariat all the same. The parson has shown unexpected power and so has the cringing to respectability. Not a single working-class candidate had a ghost of a chance, but my Lord Tumnoddy or any parvenu snob c'd have the workers' votes with pleasure.

Engels to Marx, 18 November 1868. From *Marx and Engels on Britain*, Moscow 1953, p. 545.

DOCUMENT 8   SIR JOHN SKELTON ON DISRAELI, 1867

And the potent wizard himself, with his olive complexion and coalblack eyes, and the mighty dome of his forehead (no Christian temple, be sure), is unlike any living creature one has met. I had never seen him in the daylight before, and the daylight accentuates his strangeness. The face is more like a mask than ever, and the division between him and mere mortals more marked. They say, and say truly enough, What an actor the man is! and yet the ultimate impression is of absolute sincerity and unreserve. Grant Duff will have it that he is an alien. What's England to him, or he to England? There is just where they are wrong. Whig or Radical or Tory don't matter much, perhaps; but this mightier Venice – this Imperial Republic on which the sun never sets – that vision fascinates him, or I am much mistaken. England is the Israel of his imagination, and he will be the Imperial Minister before he dies – if he gets the chance.

From G. E. Buckle and W. M. Monypenny, *Life of Benjamin Disraeli, Earl of Beaconsfield*, Murray (2 vols, rev. edn, 1929), ii, pp. 292–3.

DOCUMENT 9   DISRAELI ON CONSERVATIVE AIMS

The following is the classical statement of the aims of the Conservative Party under Disraeli, and particularly of his support for social reform. It is worth comparing, however, with Doc. 10.

Gentlemen, I have referred to what I look upon as the first object of the Tory party – namely, to maintain the institutions of the country, and reviewing what has occurred, and referring to the present temper of the times upon these subjects, I think that the Tory party, or, as I will venture to call it, the National party, has everything to encourage it. I think that the nation, tested by many and severe trials, has arrived at the conclusion which we have always maintained, that it is the first duty of England to maintain its institutions, because to them we principally ascribe the power and prosperity of the country. Gentlemen, there is another and second great object of the Tory party. If the first is to maintain the institutions of the country, the second is, in my opinion, to uphold the Empire of England. If you look to the history of this country since the advent of Liberalism – forty years ago – you will find that there has been no effort so continuous, so subtle, supported by so much energy, and carried on with so much ability and acumen, as the attempts of Liberalism to effect the disintegration of the Empire of England. Gentlemen, another great object of the Tory party, and one not inferior to the maintenance of the Empire, or the upholding of our institutions, is the elevation of the condition of the people.

Speech at the Crystal Palace, 2 June 1872.

From *Selected Speeches of the Earl of Beaconsfield*, ed. T. E. Kebbel, vol ii, 1882.

DOCUMENT 10 **DISRAELI AND SOCIAL REFORM**

R. A. Cross was Disraeli's Home Secretary 1874–80, and responsible for important social reforms.

When the Cabinet came to discuss the Queen's Speech, I was, I confess, disappointed at the want of originality shown by the Prime Minister. From all his speeches, I had quite expected that his mind was full of legislative schemes, but such did not prove to be the case; on the contrary, he had to rely on the various suggestions of his colleagues, and as they themselves had only just come into office, and that suddenly, there was some difficulty in framing the Queen's Speech.

From Viscount Cross, *A Political History*. Quoted in Smith, [112], p. 199.

DOCUMENT 11 **GLADSTONE ON THE EVILS OF 'BEACONSFIELDISM'**

The following is typical of much of Gladstone's oratory during the Midlothian Campaign 1879–80. Disraeli's government had engaged in wars against the Zulus in South Africa, and the Afghans, in 1879.

Go from South Africa to the mountains of Central Asia. Go into the lofty hills of Afghanistan, as they were last winter, and what do we there see? I fear a yet sadder sight than was to be seen in the land of the Zulu ... You have seen during last winter from time to time that from such and such a village attacks had been made upon the British forces, and that in consequence the village had been burned. Have you ever reflected on the meaning of those words? ... Those hill tribes had committed no real offence against us. We, in the pursuit of our political objects, chose to establish military positions in their country. If they resisted, would not you have done the same? And when, going forth from their villages they had resisted, what you find is this, that those who went forth were slain, and that the village is burned. Again, I say, have you considered the meaning of these words? The meaning of the burning of the village is, that the women and the children were driven forth to perish in the snows of winter. Is not that a terrible supposition? Is not that a fact which . . . rouses in you a sentiment of horror and grief, to think that the name of England, under no political necessity, but for a war as frivolous as ever was waged in the history of man, should be associated with consequences such as these? . . .

Remember the rights of the savage, as we call him. Remember that the happiness of his humble home, remember that the sanctity of life in the hill villages of Afghanistan among the winter snows, is as inviolable in the eye of Almighty God as can be your own.

Speech at the Forsters Hall, Dalkeith, 26 November 1879. From W. E. Gladstone, *Political Speeches in Scotland, November and December, 1879*, Edinburgh 1880.

DOCUMENT 12   AN OLD-TIME ELECTION AGENT

Mr Acland dabbled in all sorts of election work. He was an adept at Election addresses. He knew how to say nothing and to say it well. None of his candidates could be convicted of breaking election pledges after their election. In the pursuit of his profession he was not always on one side; I found him out on one occasion nicely. He was Tory agent for Worcester: one of his lieutenants was agent for Droitwich, but Acland pulled the strings. I made speeches against him in both constituencies, but Acland's men won . . . . He was free and generous to a fault. He could never save money, however much he earned. . . . He was a willing helper without fee or reward when the person wanting help was too poor to pay. But as regards the rich candidate, who had his own game to play, he felt justified in spoiling the Egyptians. But he never sold his Candidate; never relaxed his efforts to get him returned. The system was corrupt; that was not his fault. He advocated a better system. Parliament refused it. The candidates liked the system; why should he complain. He lived to see the change: hustings abolished, open voting driven away with the ballot carried and the Corrupt Practices Acts amended and strengthened.

Quoted in Hanham, [135], p. 238.

DOCUMENT 13   THE WORK OF A CHIEF WHIP, 1867

Glyn was Liberal Chief Whip between 1867 and 1873, following the passing of the Second Reform Act. His letter illustrates difficulties, especially financial, that faced party officials under the new electoral conditions.

'The claims upon a Fund' are as follows.

1st Registration. We have an office in London with a Secretary etc. in communication with all the local agents, giving them advice, supplying them with all forms of claims etc. etc., also doing most important work at an election in looking up the outvoters. This is supposed to be kept alive by annual subscriptions but I find £300 a year is all I get towards an expense of near £1500. I have kept this up this year as it would have been most foolish to lose all this perfect machinery (the only basis of organization which we have) upon the eve of a General election. Hayter says it costs more than it is worth but Brand has been a strong advocate for it, & I certainly now find it most necessary. I am sure we have saved thousands of votes by the information & instructions sent to local agents from our headquarters.

The 2nd expense is The Office here which it is needful to have for some months before an election, & if any one sees [? how] the daily work here runs, the visits of candidates & agents & the correspondence & telegraphs upon matters of candidates the necessity for such a 'house of call' cd. not be doubted.

The fund is wanted 3rdly for aid in some cases towards local registration & in some degree for expenses of meetings etc. to rouse popular feeling which can only be done by sending men down to aid candidates etc. etc.

4thly for direct assistance to candidates & of course here, when the money is gone, I cannot tell exactly how it goes but it is given to the candidate & upon the understanding that it is in aid of legitimate expenditure. There are many places where special men are necessary & sometimes such men may have a little less money to spend than the place will fairly cost .... I don't think it possible to manage properly without say £10000 to £15000.

Glyn to Gladstone, 12 September 1867. Quoted in Thompson, [153].

DOCUMENT 14   THE CONSERVATIVE CENTRAL OFFICE, 1880

Compared with Document 13 this shows clearly the enormous advance made in central party organisation since 1867.

ORDINARY WORK OF CONSERVATIVE CENTRAL OFFICE
Registration. Enquiries are made as to the residence and qualifications of the outvoters of all counties in England & Wales. Forms, instructions & advice are furnished to both Counties and Boroughs.
Elections. Local leaders are assisted in finding suitable candidates. Forms, instructions, and election literature is supplied. County outvoters are canvassed.
Organization. Formation of new Associations is promoted and assisted. Model

rules &c. are supplied. An annual list of clubs & associations is compiled. Meetings. The continual holding of small local meetings is advised and encouraged. Speakers and hints for speeches are provided. Special meetings (as for example on the Irish question) are from time to time recommended and promoted.

Publications. Pamphlets & Leaflets on current political topics are issued: important speeches are reprinted and circulated. Press. A weekly publication, called the 'Editors' Handysheet', is issued to provide materials for political articles to the Conservative Provincial Press. Political telegrams are sent from the Lobby to several provincial papers.

Parliamentary. All Bills affecting the interests of the party are circulated amongst the local leaders. Petitions are from time to time promoted.

Statistics. Facts respecting elections, Parliamentary & municipal, are collected and tabulated. An index of political events during the past 10 years is in course of formation.

Correspondence. Enquiries are answered upon such subjects as Finance, Foreign Affairs, Army & Navy administration, Election statistics & procedure, India, Irish affairs, Licensing, Education, Friendly Societies, &c. &c.

Interviews. People of every class call at the office on political business, and every endeavour is made to treat them with courtesy & consideration.

Visits. Constituencies are visited by emissaries from the Central Office of two sorts:

(a) Experienced agents to advise on the registration & electoral machinery.

(b) Gentlemen to stir up dormant constituencies, & recommend local organisation & effort.

J.A. Gorst to Disraeli, 24 February 1881. Quoted in Feuchtwanger, [133], p. 151.

DOCUMENT 15   J.A. GORST ON THE CONSERVATIVE
              PARTY

J. A. Gorst brilliantly reorganised the Conservative Party machine in the 1870s, but he felt that his efforts were insufficiently rewarded by the party leaders. The following extract illustrates not only his 'Tory Democracy', but personal pique.

If the Tory party is to continue to exist as a power in the State, it must become a popular party. A mere coalition with the Whig aristocracy might delay, but could not avert its downfall. The days are past when an exclusive class, however great its ability, wealth, and energy, can command a majority in the electorate. The liberties and interests of the people at large are the only things which it is now possible to conserve: the rights of property, the Established Church, the House of Lords, and the Crown itself must be defended on the ground that they are institutions necessary or useful to the preservation of civil and religious liberty and securities for personal freedom, and can be maintained only so far as the people take this view of their subsistence. Unfortunately for Conservatism, its leaders belong solely to one class; they are a clique composed of members of the aristocracy, land-owners, and adherents whose chief merit is subserviency. The party chiefs live in an atmosphere in which a sense of their own importance and of the importance of their class interests and privileges is exaggerated, and to which the opinions of the common people can scarcely penetrate. They are surrounded by sycophants who continually offer up the incense of personal flattery under the pretext of conveying political information. They half fear and half despise the common people, whom they see only through this deceptive medium; they regard them more as dangerous allies to be coaxed and cajoled than as comrades fighting for a common cause.

From 'Conservative disorganisation', *The Fortnightly Review*, vol. 32, 1882.

DOCUMENT 16   **LORD RANDOLPH CHURCHILL ON MR GLADSTONE**

This, and the following extract [Doc. 17], illustrate Lord Randolph's wit and eloquence as an orator. Clearly, he was better at destruction (and Gladstone was the perfect foil) than construction.

'Vanity of vanities,' says the preacher, 'all is vanity!' 'Humbug of humbugs,' says the Radical, 'all is humbug.' Gentlemen, we live in an age of advertisement, the age of Holloway's pills, of Colman's mustard, and of Horniman's pure tea; and the policy of lavish advertisement has been so successful in commerce that the Liberal party, with its usual enterprise, had adapted it to politics. The Prime Minister is the greatest living master of the art of personal political advertisement. Holloway, Colman, and Horniman are nothing compared with him. Every act of his, whether it be for the purposes of health, or of recreation, or of religious devotion, is spread before the eyes of every man, woman and child in the United Kingdom on large and glaring placards. For the purposes of an autumn holiday a large transatlantic steamer is specially engaged, the Poet Laureate adorns the suite and receives a peerage as his reward, and the incidents of the voyage are luncheon with the Emperor of Russia and tea with the Queen of Denmark. For the purposes of recreation he has selected the felling of trees; and we may usefully remark that his amusements, like his politics, are essentially destructive. Every afternoon the whole world is invited to assist at the crashing fall of some beech or elm or oak. The forest laments, in order that Mr Gladstone may perspire . . .

From Speech at Blackpool, 24 January 1884. Quoted in *Speeches of Lord Randolph Churchill*, ed. L. J. Jennings, Longman, 1889, i, pp. 111–12.

DOCUMENT 17   TORY DEMOCRACY

The Whigs arc a class with the prejudices and the vices of a class; the Radicals are a sect with the tyranny and the fanaticism of a sect. . . . . The Whigs tell you that the institutions of this kingdom, as illustrated by the balance of Queen, Lords, and Commons, and the Established Church, are but conveniences and useful commodities, which may be safely altered, modified, or even abolished, so long as the alteration, modification or abolition is left to the Whigs to carry out. The Radicals tell you that these institutions are hideous, poisonous and degrading, and that the divine Caucus is the only machine which can turn out, as if it was a patent medicine, the happiness of humanity. But the Tories, who are of the people, know and exclaim that these institutions, which are not so much the work of the genius of man, but rather the inspired offspring of Time, are the tried guarantees of individual liberty, popular government, and Christian morality; that they are the only institutions which possess the virtue of stability, of stability even through all ages; that the harmonious fusion of classes and interests which they represent corresponds with and satisfies the highest aspirations either of peoples or of men; that by them has our Empire been founded and extended in the past; and that by them alone can it prosper or be maintained in the future. Such is the Tory party and such are its principles, by which it can give to England the government she requires – democratic, aristocratic, Parliamentary, monarchical, uniting in an indissoluble embrace religious liberty and social order.

Speech at Blackpool, 24 January 1884. Quoted in Churchill, [92], p. 230.

DOCUMENT 18   THE NATIONAL LIBERAL FEDERATION

This, and the following two documents [19, 20], illustrate views within the Liberal Party of the 'caucus system', which may be said to date from the formation of the National Liberal Federation in 1877. Lord Hartington, the leading Whig, was at this time leader of the party.

The Federation is designed to assist the formation of Liberal Associations, on a popular representative basis, throughout the country; to bring such organisations into union, so that by this means the opinions of Liberals, on measures to be supported or resisted, may be readily and authoritatively ascertained; and to aid in concentrating upon the promotion of reforms found to be generally desired the whole force, strength, and resources of the Liberal Party.

The essential feature of the proposed Federation is the principle which must henceforth govern the action of Liberals as a political party – namely, the direct participation of all members of the party in the direction of its policy, and in the selection of those particular measures of reform and of progress to which priority shall be given. This object can be secured only by the organisation of the party upon a representative basis; that is, by popularly elected committees of local associations, and by the union of such local associations, by means of their freely chosen representatives, in a general federation.

From *Proceedings Attending the Formation of the National Federation of Liberal Associations*, Birmingham 1877.

DOCUMENT 19   CHAMBERLAIN ON THE CAUCUS

The opponents of the Caucus are not to be convinced – they hate it for its virtues – because it puts aside and utterly confounds all that club management and Pall Mall selection which has been going on for so long and which has made of the Lib Party the molluscous, boneless, nerveless thing it is. The Caucus is force, enthusiasm, zeal, activity, movement, popular will and the rule of the majority – the Seven Deadly Sins in fact.

Joseph Chamberlain to John Morley, 29 September 1878. Quoted in Garvin and Amery, [41], i, p. 262.

DOCUMENT 20   LORD HARTINGTON ON THE NATIONAL LIBERAL FEDERATION

I do not feel at all certain that we ought to give in our adhesion to this federation scheme. The Birmingham plan is perhaps the only one on which the Liberal party can be sufficiently organised in a great constituency; and I do not know whether there is much or any objection to its being extended to others. But it is almost certain to put the management into the hands of the most advanced men, because they are the most active. And when we come to a federation of these associations, it seems to me that it will come before long to placing the chief control and direction of the party in the hands of these men, to the exclusion of the more moderate and easy-going Liberals. There is a good deal of the American caucus system about it, which I think is not much liked here; and though we have all been preaching organisation, I think we may sacrifice too much to it.

Lord Hartington to Lord Granville, 23 November 1877. Quoted in Holland, [47], i, p. 245.

DOCUMENT 21   THE 'UNAUTHORISED PROGRAMME'

This extract is typical of Joseph Chamberlain's early speeches during his campaign for the 'Unauthorised Programme' (so called because it did not have the backing of Gladstone and the party leadership) in 1885. Its attack on property rights shows why Lord Salisbury denounced him as 'Jack Cade'. But in fact Chamberlain modified his ideas in the course of the campaign.

We have to account for and to grapple with the mass of misery and destitution in our midst, coexistent as it is with the evidence of abundant wealth and teeming prosperity. It is a problem which some men would put aside by references to the eternal laws of supply and demand, to the necessity of freedom of contract, and to the sanctity of every private right of property. But, gentlemen, these phrases are the convenient cant of selfish wealth. They are no answers to our question. I quite understand the reason for timidity in dealing with this matter so long as Government was merely the expression of the will and prejudice of a limited few. Under such circumstances there might be good reason for not intrusting it with larger powers, even for the relief of this misery and destitution. But now that we have a Government of the people by the people, we will go on and make it the Government for the people, in which all shall cooperate in order to secure to every man his natural rights, his right to existence, and to a fair enjoyment of it. I shall be told tomorrow that this is Socialism. I have learnt not to be afraid of words that are flung in my face instead of argument. Of course it is Socialism. The Poor Law is Socialism; the Education Act is Socialism; the greater part of municipal work is Socialism; and every kindly act of legislation, by which the community has sought to discharge its responsibilities and its obligations to the poor is Socialism; but it is none the worse for that. Our object is the elevation of the poor, of the masses of the people – a levelling up of them by which we shall do something to remove the excessive inequality in social life which is now one of the greatest dangers as well as a great injury to the State.

Speech at Warrington, 8 September 1885.
From *Speeches of Right Hon. Joseph Chamberlain, M.P.* ed. H. W. Lucy, 1885.

DOCUMENT 22   GLADSTONE AND IRISH NATIONALITY

It was during the summer months of 1885 that Gladstone, privately, became converted to the necessity for Home Rule for Ireland. A major reason for this was his growing conviction of the reality of Irish nationalism, and his belief that his previous policies of reform and coercion had failed. This may be compared with Chamberlain's views [Doc. 23]; and the light thrown on his attitude towards the Home Rule Bill of 1886 by Doc. 24.

He (Gladstone) said he had been studying the subject a good deal; that he had come to the conclusion that the Union was a mistake; that Pitt had assigned no sufficient justification for destroying the national life of Ireland; that he did not hold the popular theory that a single executive could not co-exist with two independent legislatures (witness Norway and Sweden, Austria and Hungary); he did not believe the Irish irreconcilable; thought they would have accepted moderate terms till R. Churchill came into power; now nothing less than a Parliament of their own would satisfy them; the question was becoming urgent; the Irish were better organised than ever; we could not go on with eighty or ninety of them in the House of Commons – the state of that body now was a disgrace, and it would be worse in the new Parliament.

Lord Derby to Earl Granville, 2 October 1885. Quoted in Garvin and Amercy, [41], ii, p. iii.

DOCUMENT 23   CHAMBERLAIN ON IRELAND

I hate coercion; but I loathe violence and disorder more. I do not judge the morality of Irish proceedings but I recognise facts. We are in a state of war, and I will use every conceivable means to come out victorious. They mean to destroy the Government, and perhaps in this they may be successful. They want also to make all government of Ireland by England impossible, and in this they will assuredly fail, as all our people, Radicals included, will resist them to the death.

Joseph Chamberlain to John Morley, 18 December 1881. Quoted in Garvin and Amercy, [41], ii, p. 345.

DOCUMENT 24   CHAMBERLAIN AND HOME RULE

The immediate result will be considerable unpopularity and temporary estrangement from the Radical Party. There is little backbone in politics and the great majority are prepared to swallow anything and to stick to the machine. In the Cabinet I have no support worth mentioning. . . . I shall be left almost alone for a time. I cannot, of course, work with the Tories, and Hartington is quite as much hostile to my radical views as to W.G.'s Irish plans. But in time the situation will clear. Either Mr. Gladstone will succeed and get the Irish question out of the way, or he will fail. In either case he will retire from politics and I do not suppose the Liberal Party will accept Childers or even John Morley as its permanent leader.

Joseph Chamberlain to Arthur Chamberlain, 8 March 1886. Quoted in Hurst, [123], p. 14.

DOCUMENT 25 THE WORKING CLASS AND LIBERALISM

Sidney Webb was at this time a young civil servant, active in London politics. The view expressed is probably true of the whole period 1886 to 1900.

The general tone of mind and bias of character of the London wage-earner is emphatically Radical. Nevertheless it is by no means uncommon for them to vote by hundreds for the Conservative candidate, partly from sheer disgust at the weakness of Liberalism, partly no doubt because of specious 'Tory Democratic' promises, but mainly for personal or accidental reasons. ... Their usual attitude, however, is abstention; first from registration; then, if registered, perforce, from the polling-booth. Practically none of them give any assistance in ordinary times to the necessary work of a Liberal Association. Even such of them as can be induced at the election to vote for the Liberal candidate, are in the party but not of it. There is an almost universal conviction among them that its aims are not theirs, and that its representatives are not those whom they would have chosen.

From Sidney Webb, *Wanted a Programme: An Appeal to the Liberal Party,* *1888.* Quoted from Simon Maccoby, *English Radicalism 1886–1914,* Allen & Unwin 1953, pp. 58–9.

DOCUMENT 26 GLADSTONE'S LAST CABINET, MARCH 1894

The Earl of Kimberley was, in 1894, Foreign Secretary, and had served in Liberal governments continuously since 1868. The Chancellor of the Exchequer was Sir William Harcourt.

On March 1 Mr Gladstone held his last Cabinet. After the business was concluded Kimberley said that he could not allow our meeting to terminate without saying in a word how painful it was for us to part with our chief, and in a moment the honest old fellow was sobbing, unable to proceed. Mr G. was about to reply when a cry of 'Stop!' was heard. It was the Chancellor of the Exchequer. As soon as he had arrested Mr G.'s attention he pulled from his pocket a handkerchief and a manuscript and at once commenced weeping loudly. Then he said, 'I think I can best express my feelings by reading the letter I have addressed to you, Sir, on this occasion' – on which he declaimed to us a somewhat pompous valedictory address of which I only remember vaguely a long-drawn metaphor taken from the solar system. Mr Gladstone was obviously disgusted. He said a few cold words, and always referred to this Cabinet as 'the blubbering Cabinet'.

From the Earl of Rosebery, 'Mr Gladstone's Last Cabinet', [72].

DOCUMENT 27   ROSEBERY'S POSITION AS PRIME
MINISTER

The Liberal government of 1892–95 was dependent for its parliamentary
majority on the Irish Party. The leader of the Liberal Party in the House of
Commons after Gladstone's retirement was Sir William Harcourt,
previously Rosebery's rival for the succession to Gladstone, and his personal
enemy.

He is as Prime Minister more unfortunately situated than any man who ever
held that high office. He has inherited from his predecessor a policy, a
Cabinet, and a Parliament; besides a party of groups, one of which is aimed
against himself. All this is kept in existence by a narrow majority which
may at any moment break away. He himself is only able to guide this
tumultuous party through a leader, bitterly hostile to himself, and
ostentatiously indifferent to the fate of the Government.

Lord Rosebery in the meantime is shut up in a House almost
unanimously opposed to his ministry, and, for all political purposes, might
as well be in the Tower of London.

Earl of Rosebery to Queen Victoria, 14 May 1894. Quoted in Hanham, [8],
pp. 71–2.

DOCUMENT 28   ASQUITH ON THE LIBERAL PARTY, 1898

Asquith was Home Secretary 1892–95 and, though his political sympathies
lay more with Rosebery than Harcourt, his view of the Liberal Party is
reasonably objective. He was himself a possible candidate for the party
leadership in 1898 after the retirement of Harcourt.

The new birth has not yet come, nor is there anything in the heavens above
or in the earth beneath to portend the event. Harcourt's leadership excites
no enthusiasm, and, in view of his age & of the other conditions, is
probably regarded by the bulk of the people as a merely provisional
arrangement. There is a disposition – I think a growing one – to turn to
Rosebery, but there are many who cannot forget or forgive his timely
escape, in a life-boat constructed to hold one person, from the water-logged
ship. And for the moment there is no one else whose name is even generally
acceptable, let alone a rallying cry for a broken army. The fact is that
people have been so accustomed for more than a generation upon both
sides to leaders who are obviously marked out for the post (Palmerston,
Gladstone, Disraeli, Salisbury) that they are bewildered by the problem of
choice. In the end it will no doubt solve itself by the action of natural

forces, but in the meantime the effectiveness of the party as a political instrument is crippled.

H.H. Asquith to Alfred Milner, January 1898. Quoted in Stansky, [77], p. 234.

DOCUMENT 29   **LABOUR AND THE CAUCUS**

Threlfall was a trade union leader and active worker for greater labour representation in Parliament. His views are typical of those of many labour leaders in the later nineteenth century.

Theoretically the caucus is a perfect machine, but in practice it is one-sided ... It is only a waste of time to advise the working classes to attend and make the caucus what they want it to be. The fact is they distrust it – they regard it as a middle-class machine; they have neither the time nor the inclination to compete with the wire-pullers who work it, and they have a decided objection to being made the puppets of anyone. It has served its purpose, and it has carried the people through one state of their development: but as it exists today it is too narrow and too much hampered with class prejudice to be a reflex of the expanding democratic and labour sentiment.

T. R. Threlfall in *The Nineteenth Century*, February 1894. Quoted in Pelling, [169], pp. 222–3.

DOCUMENT 30   **SALISBURY ON LORD RANDOLPH CHURCHILL, 1886**

Lord Cranbrook, Lord President of the Council, complained to Salisbury about his undue regard for Churchill's opinions. The Prime Minister's reply reveals his true feelings.

What you call my self-renunciation is merely an effort to deal with an abnormal and very difficult state of things. It arises from the peculiarities of Churchill. Beach having absolutely refused to lead, Churchill is the only possible leader in the House of Commons – and his ability is unquestionable. But he is wholly out of sympathy with the rest of the Cabinet, and, being besides of a wayward and headstrong disposition, he is far from mitigating his resistance by the method of it. As his office of Leader of the House gives him a claim to be heard on every question, the machine is moving along with the utmost friction both in home and foreign affairs. My self-renunciation is only an attempt – a vain attempt – to pour oil upon the creaking and groaning machinery. Like you, I am penetrated with a sense of the danger which the collapse of the Government would bring about: otherwise I should not have undertaken – or should have quickly abandoned – the task of leading an orchestra in which the first fiddle plays one tune and everybody else, including myself, wishes to play another.

Lord Salisbury to Lord Cranbrook, November 1886. Quoted in James, [103], p. 277.

DOCUMENT 31   THE LIBERAL UNIONIST PARTY

This extract from Joseph Chamberlain's Political Memoir (written mainly in 1892 in defence of his policies over the previous ten years) well illustrates his difficulties as a Liberal Unionist after 1887.

All attempts at reconciliation and the reunion of the Liberal Party having now failed, the next few years, from 1888 till the General Election of 1892, were occupied in maintaining and strengthening the Unionist alliance. The situation was extremely difficult – especially at first. The Conservative Party had their old traditions and methods and were inclined to move slowly or not at all. Lord Hartington, who in 1885 had been the most moderate of Whigs, found little difficulty in accepting a negative policy. He showed no initiative and was inclined on all occasions to wait for the Tory lead and at the same time was most destructive in his criticisms of all new proposals and policies. On the other hand the Liberal Unionists in the country were restive at the idea of working with, and especially under, new allies. They had been accustomed to look on all that bore the name, or was connected with the idea, of Toryism as altogether unacceptable and detestable. They were determined not to sacrifice their Liberalism, and were pledged to reforms which they had hitherto been accustomed to identify with the Liberal Party. Unless this important section of Liberals, whose sole difference with Mr Gladstone was the Home Rule question, and who were eager to find a compromise on this, could be kept true, the Gladstonians would speedily outnumber the Conservatives in the country, and would return to power with a majority sufficient to carry their policy. The position of Liberal Unionists in the constituencies was not a pleasant one. They were reviled by their former friends, and did not thoroughly trust, nor were they trusted by, their new allies. They were without efficient organisation, isolated and uneasy; and accordingly many did go back to their old party as the by-elections showed; while others, less strongly Liberal in their convictions, frankly joined the Tories, ceasing to call themselves Liberals at all.

Quoted in Chamberlain, [32], pp. 276–7.

DOCUMENT 32   CHAMBERLAIN ON THE SOCIALIST
MENACE

This extract shows how far Chamberlain had travelled in his social and
political views since 1885. It may be compared with Doc. 21.

Information obtained from a great number of constituencies . . . and
confirmed by other correspondence, shows that the electors are much more
interested at the present time in social questions and the problems connected
with the agitations of the Labour Party than they are in either the House of
Lords or any other constitutional subject. There is much more searching of
heart among the most moderate, and above all the wealthier Gladstonians.
The men who have anything to lose are getting uneasy now that they see
that Gladstonianism is not likely to be confined to an attack upon Irish
landlords or British millionaires, but will probably result in an onslaught on
capital generally.

The resolutions of the TUC . . . amount to universal confiscation in order
to create a Collectivist State. It is true that this is at present an unauthorised
programme, but the policy of the Gladstonian leaders has been, and still is,
to invite popular pressure in order that they may yield to it . . . in doing so,
they will risk a further secession of all that remains to them of wealth,
intelligence, and moderation.

From Joseph Chamberlain, *Memorandum*, November 1894. Quoted in
Fraser, [121], pp. 64–5.

DOCUMENT 33   THE 'HOTEL CECIL'

Salisbury's last ministry contained two of his nephews – Gerald and Arthur
Balfour – hence the nickname of the 'Hotel Cecil'. Bartley had been
Conservative party agent 1882–85.

It becomes clearer after every appointment that though men may work their
hearts out and make every sacrifice financial and otherwise when the
Conservative party is in opposition and in difficulties, yet in prosperous
times all is forgotten and all honours, emoluments and places are reserved
for the friends and relations of the favoured few, many of whom were in the
nursery while some of us were fighting uphill battles for the party.

G. C. T. Bartley to Lord Salisbury, 22 October 1898. Quoted in Cornford,
[95], p. 268.

DOCUMENT 34   LORD SALISBURY ON THE
CONSERVATIVE PARTY

Salisbury's reply to Lord Randolph Churchill's demand for a more vigorous reform policy illustrates perfectly his slow, cautious, sceptical view of political change.

For the rest, I fully see all the difficulties of our position. The Tory party is composed of very varying elements, and there is merely trouble and vexation of spirit in trying to make them work together. I think the 'classes and the dependants of class' are the strongest ingredients in our composition, but we have so to conduct our legislation that we shall give some satisfaction to both classes and masses. This is specially difficult with the classes – because all legislation is rather unwelcome to them, as tending to disturb a state of things with which they are satisfied. It is evident, therefore, that we must work at less speed and at a lower temperature than our opponents. Our Bills must be tentative and cautious, not sweeping and dramatic. But I believe that with patience, feeling our way as we go, we may yet get the one element to concede and the other to forbear. The opposite course is to produce drastic, symmetrical measures, hitting the 'classes' hard, and consequently dispensing with their support, but trusting to public meetings and the democratic forces generally to carry you through. I think such a policy will fail. I do not mean that the 'classes' will join issue with you on one of the measures which hits them hard, and beat you on that. That is not the way they fight. They will select some other matter on which they can appeal to prejudice, and on which they think the masses will be indifferent; and on that they will upset you.

Lord Salisbury to Lord Randolph Churchill, 7 November 1886. Quoted in Churchill, [92], p. 565.

BIBLIOGRAPHY

GENERAL

1 Adelman, Paul. *Victorian Radicalism*, Longman, 1984.
2 Beales, Derek. *From Castlereagh to Gladstone 1815–1885*, Nelson, 1969.
3 Bebbington, D. W. *The Nonconformist Conscience: Chapel and Politics 1870–1914*, Allen and Unwin, 1982.
4 Clarke, Peter. *A Question of Leadership. From Gladstone to Thatcher*, H. Hamilton, 1991; Penguin Books, 1992.
5 Ensor, R. C. K. *England 1870–1914*, Oxford University Press, 1936: the standard textbook – and a very good one – now somewhat out of date.
6 Feuchtwanger, E. J. *Democracy and Empire. Britain 1865–1914*, Edward Arnold, 1985.
7 Halévy, Elie. *Imperialism and the Rise of Labour 1895–1905: A History of the English People in the Nineteenth Century*, vol. v, Benn, 1926: an illuminating detailed study by a great historian.
8 Hanham, H. J. *The Nineteenth Century Constitution. Documents and Commentary*, Cambridge University Press, 1969: almost the only documentary collection that covers this period.
9 Kitson Clark, G. *An Expanding Society. Britain 1830–1900*, Cambridge University Press, 1967.
10 Koss, Stephen. *The Rise and Fall of the Political Press in Britain, Vol. 1, The Nineteenth Century*, H. Hamilton, 1981.
11 Pugh, Martin. *The Making of Modern British Politics 1867–1939*, Blackwell, 1982.
12 Read, Donald. *England 1868–1914: The Age of Urban Democracy*, Longman, 1979.
13 Shannon, Richard. *The Crisis of Imperialism 1865–1915*, Hart-Davis, McGibbon, 1974; Paladin edn, 1976: strong on ideas.
14 Taylor, A. J. P. *Essays in English History*, Penguin Books, 1976.

For the earlier Victorian period:

15 Bagehot, Walter. *The English Constitution*, 2nd edn, 1872; Oxford University Press, 1928: a classic study of the mid-Victorian constitution.

16   Burn, W. L. *The Age of Equipoise*, Allen & Unwin, 1964.
17   Cowling, Maurice, *1867: Disraeli, Gladstone and Revolution*,
      Cambridge University Press, 1967.
18   Gilbert, Alan D. *Religion and Society in Industrial England*,
      Longman, 1976.
19   Kitson Clark, G. *The Making of Victorian England*, Methuen, 1962.
20   Machin, G. I. T. *Politics and the Churches in Great Britain 1832 to
      1868*, Oxford University Press, 1977.
21   Smith, F. B. *The Making of the Second Reform Bill*, Cambridge
      University Press, 1966.

THE LIBERAL PARTY

22   Adams, Francis. *History of the Elementary School Contest in
      England*, Chapman & Hall, 1882: important for the
      'Nonconformist Revolt'.
23   Adelman, Paul. *The Decline of the Liberal Party 1910–1931*,
      Seminar Studies in History, Longman, 1982. (2nd edn, 1995).
24   Barker, Michael. *Gladstone and Radicalism. The Reconstruction of
      Liberal Policy in Britain 1885–1894*, The Harvester Press, 1975.
25   Beckett, J. C. *The Making of Modern Ireland 1603–1923*, Faber,
      1966.
26   Bentley, Michael. *The Climax of Liberal Politics. British Liberalism
      in Theory and Practice 1868–1918*, Edward Arnold, 1987.
27   Biagini, Eugenio, F. 'Popular Liberals, Gladstonian finance, and the
      debate on taxation, 1860–1874', in *Currents of Radicalism.
      Popular Radicalism, Organised Labour and Party Politics in Britain
      1850–1914*, ed. Eugenio F. Biagini and Alastair J. Reid, Cambridge
      University Press, 1991.
28   Biagini, Eugenio, F. *Liberty, Retrenchment and Reform. Popular
      Liberalism in the Age of Gladstone 1860–1880*, Cambridge
      University Press, 1992.
29   Butler, Jeffrey. *The Liberal Party and the Jameson Raid*, Oxford
      University Press, 1968.
30   Chamberlain, Joseph. 'The Liberal Party and its leaders', *Fortnightly
      Review*, vol. 14, 1873.
31   Chamberlain, Joseph. Preface to *The Radical Programme*, 1885.
32   Chamberlain, Joseph. *A Political Memoir 1880–92*, ed. C. H. D.
      Howard, Batchworth Press, 1953: an apologia.
33   Clarke, P. F. *Lancashire and the New Liberalism*, Cambridge
      University Press, 1971.
34   Cook, Chris. *A Short History of the Liberal Party 1900–1976*,
      Macmillan, 1976.

35 Cooke, A. B. and Vincent, John. *The Governing Passion. Cabinet Government and Party Politics in Britain 1885–86*, The Harvester Press, 1974: a study of 'high (often stratospheric) politics'.

36 Douglas, Roy. *History of the Liberal Party 1895–1970*, Sidgwick and Jackson, 1971.

37 Emy, H. V. *Liberals, Radicals and Social Politics 1892–1914*, Cambridge University Press, 1973.

38 Escott, T. H. S. 'The revolution of 1884', *Fortnightly Review*, vol. 37, 1885.

39 Feuchtwanger, E. J. *Gladstone*, Allen Lane, 1975. (2nd edn, Macmillan, 1989).

40 Fraser, Peter. *Joseph Chamberlain*, Cassell, 1966.

41 Garvin, J. L. and Amery, Julian. *Life of Joseph Chamberlain*, 6 vols, Macmillan, 1932–69: the standard life.

42 Glaser, John F. 'English nonconformists and the decline of Liberalism', *American Historical Review*, vol. 63, 1957–58.

43 Hamer, D. A. *John Morley. Liberal Intellectual in Politics*, Oxford University Press, 1968.

44 Hamer, D. A. *Liberal Politics in the Age of Gladstone and Rosebery*, Oxford University Press, 1972: the outstanding study of the late Victorian Liberal Party.

45 Hammond, J. L. *Gladstone and the Irish Nation* (1st edn, 1938), Cass, 1964: the standard work – very pro-Gladstone.

46 Hilton, Boyd. 'Gladstone's theological politics', in *High and Low Politics in Modern Britain*, ed. Michael Bentley and John Stevenson, Oxford University Press, 1983.

47 Holland, Bernard. *The Life of Spencer Compton, 8th Duke of Devonshire*, 2 vols, Longmans, 1911.

48 Howard, C. H. D. 'Joseph Chamberlain and the "Unauthorised Programme"', *English Historical Review*, vol. 65, 1950.

49 Jagger, Peter, ed. *Gladstone, Politics and Religion*, Macmillan, 1985.

50 James, R. R. *Rosebery*, Weidenfeld & Nicolson, 1963.

51 Jay, Richard. *Joseph Chamberlain. A Political Study*, Oxford University Press, 1988.

52 Jenkins, Roy. *Gladstone*, Macmillan, 1995.

53 Jenkins, T. A. *Gladstone, Whiggery and the Liberal Party 1874–1886*, Oxford University Press, 1988.

54 Jenkins, T. A. *The Liberal Ascendancy, 1830–1886*, Macmillan, 1994.

55 Judd, Denis. *Radical Joe. A Life of Joseph Chamberlain*, Hamish Hamilton, 1977.

56 Lubenow, W. C. 'Irish Home Rule and the great separation in the Liberal Party in 1886: the dimensions of parliamentary Liberalism', *Victorian Studies*, vol. 26, 1982–83.

57 Lyons, F. S. L. *Ireland since the Famine*, Weidenfeld and Nicolson, 1971.

118   *Bibliography*

58   Machin, G. I. T. 'Gladstone and nonconformity in the 1860s: the formation of an alliance', *The Historical Journal*, vol. xvii, 1974.
59   Magnus, Philip. *Gladstone*, Murray, 1954.
60   Marsh, Peter T. *Joseph Chamberlain. Entrepreneur in Politics*, Yale University Press, 1994.
61   Matthew, H. C. G. *The Liberal Imperialists*, Oxford University Press, 1973.
62   Matthew, H. C. G., ed. *The Gladstone Diaries*, vol. V, 1855–1860, Oxford University Press, 1978: contains an illuminating introduction.
63   Matthew, H. C. G. vol. 1, *Gladstone 1809–1874*; vol. 2, *Gladstone 1875–1898*, Oxford University Press, 1986, 1995.
64   McCready, H. W. 'Home Rule and the Liberal Party 1899–1906', *Irish Historical Studies*, vol. 13, 1962–63.
65   Morgan, Kenneth O. *The Age of Lloyd George. The Liberal Party and British Politics 1890–1929*, Allen and Unwin, 1971.
66   Morley, John. *Life of Gladstone*, 2 vols, Macmillan, 1905 edn.
67   Parry, J. P. 'Religion and the collapse of Gladstone's first government, 1870–1874', *The Historical Journal*, vol. xxv, 1982.
68   Parry, J. P. *Democracy and Religion. Gladstone and the Liberal Party 1867–1875*, Cambridge University Press, 1986; paperback edn, 1989.
69   Parry, Jonathan. *The Rise and Fall of Liberal Government in Victorian Britain*, Yale University Press, 1993.
70   Ramm, Agatha, ed. *The Political Correspondence of Mr Gladstone and Lord Granville 1876–1886*, 2 vols, Oxford University Press, 1962: contains a valuable introduction.
71   Ramm, Agatha. *William Ewart Gladstone*, GPC Books, Wales University Press, 1989.
72   Rosebery, Earl of. 'Mr Gladstone's last cabinet', *History Today*, Dec. 1951 and Jan. 1952: an important contemporary document.
73   Shannon, R. T. *Gladstone and the Bulgarian Agitation 1876*, Nelson, 1963: an outstanding book, with wider implications than its title suggests.
74   Shannon, Richard. *Gladstone, Vol. 1 1809–1865*, H. Hamilton 1982; Methuen University Paperback, 1984.
75   Shannon, Richard. 'Gladstone and Home Rule 1886', in *Ireland after the Union*, with an introduction by Lord Blake, Oxford University Press, 1989.
76   Southgate, Donald. *The Passing of the Whigs 1832–1886*, Macmillan, 1962: together with 47 it provides a full–dress portrait of the Whig section of the Liberal Party.
77   Stansky, Peter. *Ambitions and Struggles. The Struggle for the Leadership of the Liberal Party in the 1890's*, Oxford University Press, 1964: a detailed study of the 'in-fighting' – only for addicts.

78 Steele, E. D. 'Gladstone and Ireland', *Irish Historical Studies*, vol. 17, 1970–71.

79 Thompson, A. F. 'Gladstone', *History Today*, November 1952: a hostile view.

80 Vincent, John. *The Formation of the Liberal Party 1857–1868*, Constable 1965: a brilliant, stimulating and exasperating book.

81 Vincent, John. 'Gladstone and Ireland', *Proceedings of the British Academy*, vol. 63, 1977.

82 Williams, W. E. *The Rise of Gladstone to the Leadership of the Liberal Party 1859–1868*, Cambridge University Press, 1934.

83 Wilson, Trevor. *The Downfall of the Liberal Party 1914–1935*, Collins (Fontana Library edn), 1968: contains an important introduction on the general problem of Liberal decline.

THE CONSERVATIVE PARTY

84 Blake, Robert. *Disraeli*, Methuen, 1966: one of the outstanding political biographies of our time.

85 Blake, Robert. *The Conservative Party from Peel to Churchill*, Eyre and Spottiswoode, 1970.

86 Blake, Lord (Robert), and Cecil, Hugh. *Salisbury. The Man and his Policies*, Macmillan, 1987.

87 Butler, Lord, ed. *The Conservatives. A History from their Origins to 1965*, Allen and Unwin, 1977.

88 Cecil, Lady Gwendolen. *Life of Robert, Marquis of Salisbury*, 4 vols, Hodder & Stoughton, 1921–32: the standard biography, but only reaches 1892.

89 Cecil, Robert. 'The past and future of Conservative policy', *Quarterly Review*, vol. 127, Oct. 1869.

90 Chilston, Viscount. *Chief Whip. The Political Life and Times of Aretas Akers-Douglas, 1st Viscount Chilston*, Routledge, 1961: this work and 91 give an excellent account of the internal workings of the Conservative Party in the later nineteenth century.

91 Chilston, Viscount. *W. H. Smith*, Routledge, 1965.

92 Churchill, W. S. *Lord Randolph Churchill* (1st edn, 1906), Odhams Press edn, 1952.

93 Coleman, Bruce. *Conservatism and the Conservative Party in Nineteenth-century Britain*, Edward Arnold, 1988.

94 Cornford, J. P. 'The transformation of Conservatism in the late 19th century', *Victorian Studies*, vol. 7, 1963–64: an outstanding article.

95 Cornford, J. P. 'The parliamentary foundations of the Hotel Cecil', in *Ideas and Institutions of Victorian England*, ed. Robert Robson, Bell, 1967.

96 Curtis, L. P. Jr. *Coercion and Conciliation in Ireland 1880–1892*, Princeton University Press, 1962.

97   Dunbabin, J. P. D. 'The politics of the establishment of county councils', *The Historical Journal*, vol. 6, 1963.

98   Elridge, C. C. *England's Mission: The Imperial Idea in the Age of Gladstone and Disraeli 1868–80*, Hodder and Stoughton, 1973.

99   Foster, R. F. *Lord Randolph Churchill. A Political Life*, Oxford University Press, 1981; paperback edn, 1988.

100   Ghosh, P. R. 'Style and substance in Disraelian social reform, c. 1860–80', in *Political and Social Change in Modern Britain*, ed. P. J. Waller, The Harvester Press, 1987.

101   Harcourt, Freda. 'Disraeli's Imperialism, 1866–1868: a question of timing', *The Historical Journal*, vol. 23, 1980.

102   Howard, C. H. D. 'Lord Randolph Churchill', *History*, vol. 25, June 1940: hostile.

103   James, Robert Rhodes. *Lord Randolph Churchill*, Weidenfeld & Nicolson, 1959: a fine modern biography, admirably complements 92.

104   Lewis, Clyde J. 'Theory and expediency in the policy of Disraeli', *Victorian Studies*, vol. 4, 1960–61.

105   Machin, Ian. *Disraeli*, Longman, 1995.

106   Marsh, Peter. *The Discipline of Popular Government: Lord Salisbury's Domestic Statecraft, 1881–1902*, The Harvester Press, 1978: a large-scale narrative.

107   McDowell, R. B. *British Conservatism 1832–1914*, Faber, 1959.

108   Pugh, Martin. *The Tory Party and the People 1880–1935*, Blackwell, 1985.

109   Quinault, R. E. 'Lord Randolph Churchill and Tory Democracy, 1880–1885', *The Historical Journal*, vol. 22, 1979.

110   Shannon, Richard. *The Age of Disraeli 1868–1881: The Rise of Tory Democracy*, Longman, 1992.

111   Shannon, Richard. *The Age of Salisbury. The Conservative Party 1881–1902*, Longman, 1996.

112   Smith, Paul. *Disraelian Conservatism and Social Reform*, Routledge, 1967.

113   Smith, Paul, ed. *Lord Salisbury on Politics*, Cambridge University Press, 1972: contains a brilliant introduction.

114   Southgate, Donald. 'The Salisbury Era 1881–1902', in *The Conservative Leadership*, ed. Donald Southgate, Macmillan, 1974.

115   Stewart, Robert. *The Foundation of the Conservative Party 1830–1867. A History of the Conservative Party*, vol 1, Longman, 1978.

116   Swartz, Marvin. *The Politics of British Foreign Policy in the Era of Disraeli and Gladstone*, Macmillan, 1985.

117   Taylor, Robert. *Lord Salisbury*, Allen Lane, 1975.

118   Vincent, John. *Disraeli*, Past Masters Series, Oxford University Press, 1990.

119   Walton, John K. *Disraeli,* (Lancaster Pamphlets) Routledge, 1990.
120   Ward, J. T. 'Derby and Disraeli', in *The Conservative Leadership*, ed.
      Donald Southgate, Macmillan, 1974.

LIBERAL UNIONISM

121   Fraser, Peter. 'The Liberal Unionist alliance: Chamberlain,
      Hartington and the Conservatives 1886–1904', *English Historical
      Review*, vol. 77, 1962.
122   Goodman, Gordon L. 'Liberal Unionism: the revolt of the Whigs',
      Victorian Studies, vol. 3, 1959.
123   Hurst, M. C. *Joseph Chamberlain and West Midland Politics
      1886–1895*. Dugdale Society Occasional Papers No. 15, Oxford
      University Press, 1962.
124   Hurst, M. C. 'Joseph Chamberlain, the Conservatives and the
      succession to John Bright 1886–1889', *The Historical Journal*, vol.
      7, 1964.
125   Hurst, M. C. *Joseph Chamberlain and Liberal Reunion*, Routledge,
      1967: important, though difficult.

ELECTIONS AND PARTY ORGANISATION

126   Beer, Samuel H. *Modern British Politics*, Faber, 1965.
127   Blewett, Neal. 'The Franchise in the United Kingdom 1885–1918',
      Past and Present, vol. 32, 1965: of major importance for the
      post-1885 period.
128   Chadwick, Mary, E. J. 'The role of redistribution in the making of
      the Third Reform Act', *The Historical Journal*, vol. 19, 1976.
129   Chamberlain, Joseph. 'A new political organisation', *Fortnightly
      Review*, vol. 22, 1877.
130   Clarke, P. F. 'The electoral sociology of modern Britain', *History*,
      vol. 57, 1972.
131   Dunbabin, J. P. D. 'Expectations of the new county councils, and
      their realization', *The Historical Journal*, vol. 8,1965.
132   Dunbabin, J. P. D. 'Parliamentary elections in Great Britain,
      1868–1900: a psephological note', *English Historical Review*, vol.
      81, 1966.
133   Feuchtwanger, E. J. *Disraeli, Democracy and the Tory Party.
      Conservative Leadership and Organisation after the Second Reform
      Bill*, Oxford University Press, 1968.
134   Fraser, Derek. *Urban Politics in Victorian England*, Leicester
      University Press, 1976.
135   Hanham, H. J. *Elections and Party Management. Politics in the time
      of Disraeli and Gladstone*, Longmans, 1959: the most important
      book for the period up to 1885.

136   Hanham, H. J. *The Reformed Electoral System in Great Britain 1832–1914,* The Historical Association, 1968: a good brief outline.
137   Herrick, Francis H. 'The origins of the National Liberal Federation', *Journal of Modern History,* vol. 17, 1945.
138   Herrick, Francis H. 'Lord Randolph Churchill and the popular organisation of the Conservative Party', *Pacific Historical Review,* vol. 15, 1946.
139   Howarth, Janet. 'The Liberal revival in Northamptonshire 1880–1895: a case study in late 19th century elections', *The Historical Journal,* vol. 12, 1969.
140   Jones, Andrew. *The Politics of Reform 1884,* Cambridge University Press, 1972.
141   Lloyd, Trevor. 'Uncontested seats in British general elections 1852–1910', *The Historical Journal,* vol. 8, 1965.
142   Lloyd, Trevor. *The General Election of 1880,* Oxford University Press, 1968.
143   Lowell, Lawrence A. *The Government of England,* 2 vols, Macmillan, 1912 edn: a near-contemporary view of the later nineteenth-century constitution.
144   Maehl, W. H. 'Gladstone, the Liberals and the election of 1874', *Bulletin of the Institute of Historical Research,* vol. 36, 1963.
145   McGill, Barry. 'Francis Schnadhorst and Liberal Party organisation', *Journal of Modern History,* vol. 35, 1962.
146   McKenzie, Robert. *British Political Parties,* 2nd edn, Heinemann, 1963: a modern classic, with important historical sections.
147   O'Leary, Cornelius. *The Elimination of Corrupt Practices in British Elections 1868–1911,* Oxford University Press, 1962.
148   Ostrogorski, M. *Democracy and the Organisation of Political Parties,* vol. 1, England, 1st edn, 1902, edited and abridged by Seymour Martin Lipset, Quadrangle Books, Chicago, 1964: a classic study of the rise of mass politics.
149   Pelling, Henry. *Social Geography of British Elections 1885–1910,* Macmillan, 1967: a pioneer study, though its methods have been much criticised.
150   Seymour, Charles, *Electoral Reform in England and Wales,* Yale University Press, 1915: still the standard work for the period up to 1885.
151   Simon, Alan. 'Church disestablishment as a factor in the general election of 1885', *The Historical Journal,* vol. 18, 1975.
152   Tholfsen, Trygve R. 'The origins of the Birmingham caucus', *The Historical Journal,* vol. 2, 1959.
153   Thompson, A. F. 'Gladstone's Whips and the general election of 1868', *English Historical Review,* vol. 63, 1948.
154   Vincent, J. R. *Pollbooks: How Victorians Voted,* Cambridge University Press, 1967.
155   Wright, D. G. *Democracy and Reform 1815–1885,* Seminar Studies in History, Longman, 1970.

ECONOMIC AND SOCIAL DEVELOPMENTS

156 Brown, B. H. *The Tariff Reform Movement in Great Britain 1881–1895*, Columbia University Press, 1943.

157 Ensor, R. C. K. 'Some political and economic interactions in later Victorian England', *Transactions of the Royal Historical Society*, vol. 31, 1949.

158 Guttsman, W. L. *The British Political Elite*, MacGibbon & Kee, 1965.

159 Hanham, H. J. 'The sale of honours in Late Victorian England', *Victorian Studies*, vol. 3, 1959–60.

160 Hobsbawm, E. J. *Industry and Empire. An Economic History of Britain since 1750*, Weidenfeld & Nicholson, 1968: a stimulating survey.

161 Pumphrey, Ralph E. 'The introduction of industrialists into the British peerage: a study in adaptation of a social institution', *American Historical Review*, vol. 65, 1959–60.

162 Thompson, F. M. L. *English Landed Society in the Nineteenth Century*, Routledge, 1963: a major work – indispensable.

163 Thompson, F. M. L. 'Land and politics in England in the nineteenth century', *Transactions of the Royal Historical Society*, vol. 15, 1965.

THE LABOUR MOVEMENT

164 Bealey, Frank, and Pelling, Henry. *Labour and Politics 1900–1906*, Macmillan, 1958.

165 Clegg, H. A., Fox, Alan, and Thompson, A. F. *A History of British Trade Unionism since 1889*, vol. I: 1889–1910, Oxford University Press, 1964.

166 Harrison, Royden, *Before the Socialists. Studies in Labour and Politics 1861–1881*, Routledge, 1965.

167 MacKenzie, Robert, and Silver, Alan. *Angels in Marble: Working-class Conservatives in Urban England*, Heinemann, 1968.

168 McKibbin, Ross. *The Evolution of the Labour Party 1910–24*, Oxford University Press, 1974.

169 Pelling, Henry, *The Origins of the Labour Party 1880–1900*, 2nd edn, Oxford University Press, 1965.

170 Pelling, Henry. *Popular Politics and Society in Late Victorian Britain*, Macmillan, 1968: a stimulating series of essays.

171 Price, Richard. *An Imperial War and the British Working Class*, Routledge, 1972.

172 Roberts, B. C. *The Trades Union Congress 1868–1921*, Allen & Unwin, 1958.

173 Thompson, Paul. *Socialists, Liberals and Labour. The Struggle for London 1885–1914*, Routledge, 1967.

174 Webb, Sidney, and Webb, Beatrice. *The History of Trade Unionism*, 2nd edn, Longmans, 1920.

INDEX